WHAT A YEAR IT WAS!

1945

A walk back in time to revisit
what life was like in the year that
has special meaning for you...

Congratulations
and
Best Wishes

To *John + Louise*

From *John & Sophie Long*

DEDICATION

In loving memory of my beautiful mother, Phyllis Gsell: When the Allied victory was announced, she handed me a pot and a wooden spoon and told me to sit on the fire escape and bang the pot as it was a day for great rejoicing!

Designer • Peter Hess
Production Coordinator • Carol Davis
Researcher • Laurie Cohn

CONTENTS

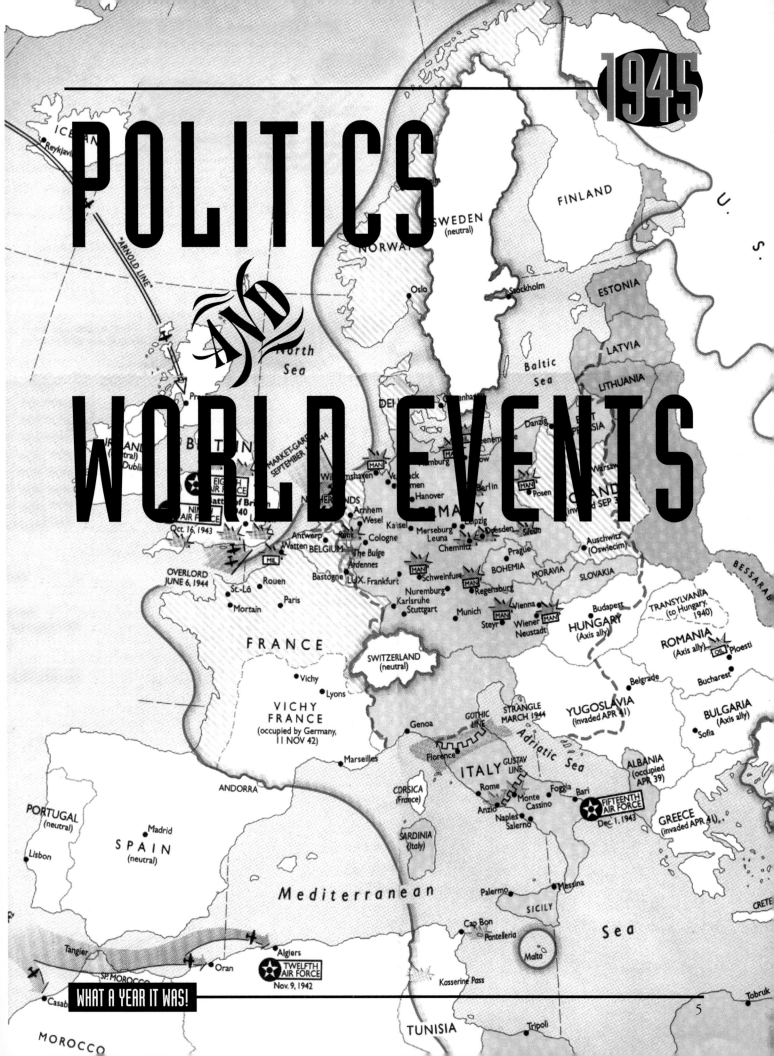

POLITICS
AND
WORLD EVENTS

WORLD WAR II

JANUARY

9	U.S. Army lands on Luzon
20	FDR inaugurated for fourth term
27	Soviet troops find 5,000 starving Jews in Auschwitz
30	Anglo-American talks prior to Yalta Conference begin at Malta

FEBRUARY

1	U.S. Rangers and Filipino guerrillas rescue American survivors of Bataan "death march"
3	U.S. Army reaches Manila
4	Yalta Conference begins (to February 12)
14	Allied planes destroy Dresden, "the Florence of Germany," home of priceless art and architectural treasures
23	U.S. Marines raise the American flag on Iwo Jima, marking victory at Mount Suribachi
23	French civilians welcome American boats arriving with food
25	B-29 raid on Tokyo demonstrates effectiveness of incendiary bombs

MARCH

3	Japanese resistance in Manila ends
7	U.S. Army crosses Rhine on bridge at Remagen
11	U.S. Eighth Army units land on Mindanao
12	Anne Frank dies at Bergen-Belsen, leaving the world her remarkable diary

APRIL

1	U.S. forces land on Okinawa
7	U.S. Navy planes sink Japanese battleship Yamato in East China Sea
9	Allies begin major attack on Gothic Line (Italy)
12	Roosevelt dies; Truman succeeds as U.S. President
18	Dachau concentration camp liberated
25	United Nations conference opens in San Francisco
28	Mussolini is executed by partisans
30	Hitler dies in bunker; Doenitz is chosen as head of state

1945

HISTORIC EVENTS

MAY

1   Joseph Goebbels commits suicide

5   German forces in Netherlands, northwestern Germany and Denmark surrender

7   All German forces surrender unconditionally (2:41 a.m. at Rheims)

8   V-E Day proclaimed

JUNE

6   Russians discover body believed to be Adolf Hitler beneath Reich Chancellery

JULY

5   MacArthur reports liberation of Philippines

14 Italy declares war on Japan

16 First atomic bomb exploded in New Mexico

17 Big Three begin Potsdam Conference (to August 2)

26 Potsdam Declaration issued

AUGUST

6   Atomic bomb dropped on Hiroshima

9   Atomic bomb dropped on Nagasaki

15 Japan surrenders at 12:00 noon Tokyo time, ending World War II

30 U.S. forces begin landing in Japan

SEPTEMBER

1   President Truman proclaims September 2 as V-J Day

2   V-J Day; Japan signs Instrument of Surrender

8   U.S. forces enter Korea to displace Japanese

9   General Douglas MacArthur takes over supervision of Japanese

11 General MacArthur orders arrest of 40 prominent Japanese civilians and military leaders on charges of war crimes

17 Josef Kramer and 44 S.S. aides go on trial in British military court to face charges of conspiracy to commit mass murder in concentration camps

25 Allies proclaim Nazi party illegal

WHAT A YEAR IT WAS!

7

SUMMARY OF HISTORIC EVENTS *(continued)*

OCTOBER

8 President Truman announces U.S. will not reveal atomic secrets to any other industrial nation

11 General MacArthur presents Premier Shidehara with five-point program for democratization of Japanese institutions

18 24 Nazi war leaders indicted on charges of plotting against world peace to face international tribunal in Nuremberg

23 President Truman recommends compulsory one year military training for U.S. youth

29 General Tomoyuki Yamashita faces war criminal charges in Manila

NOVEMBER

1 British intelligence reveals Adolf Hitler married Eva Braun on April 29 and both committed suicide the next day

13 Charles de Gaulle elected President of France

17 President Truman appoints General Eisenhower U.S. Army Chief of Staff

23 Rationing of meat, butter and all other red-point foods ends

DECEMBER

10 U.S. Strategic Bombing releases a report revealing Allied bombings killed about 500,000 German civilians, injured 700,000 and made 7,800,000 homeless

11 German industrialists who aided Hitler arrested by British authorities

15 General MacArthur issues a directive ordering the end of Shinto as the state religion of Japan

27 International Monetary Fund and Bank for Reconstruction and Development is established

WHAT A YEAR IT WAS!

"Hello Mom, It's Me!"

Of all the Long Distance calls these days, there is none that brings more joy than— "Hello Mom, it's me!"

We think those who stand aside in the evening so that service men can get their calls through faster have a very real share in the happiness that is going over the wires.

That goes, too, for those who limit their calls to five minutes when the operator requests it.

BELL TELEPHONE SYSTEM

Listen to "THE TELEPHONE HOUR" every Monday evening over NBC

9

FDR PLEDGES AN HONORABLE PEACE IN HIS INAUGURAL SPEECH

Spectators brave the winter chill to witness the inauguration of Franklin D. Roosevelt for his fourth term.

Soldiers wounded in battle are among the well-wishers on this happy occasion.

Vice President Harry S. Truman congratulates FDR after his stirring inaugural address in which he pledged an honorable and lasting peace.

FRENCH PARTISANS HELP IN WAR EFFORT

DAILY

CIRCULATION 3

With the Allies stepping up their attack on France's west front, gasoline and oil become essential to victory.

An elaborate network of pipelines is constructed through devastated villages.

WHAT A YEAR IT WAS!

From tankers on the French coast, gas is pumped directly to the front through relay storage tanks.

Loyal citizens, many of them schoolchildren, assist in the war effort by collecting the empty gas cans and returning them to various collection points for redistribution to Allied forces.

RUSSIAN DRIVE

American, British and Canadian troops use anti-tank devices in preparation for the Russian drive.

In mid-January, the British drive in Holland opens the Allied attack on the Nazi west wall.

WHAT A YEAR IT WAS!

As the Nazis retreat leaving their dead behind, German signs stand as a mocking tribute to their premature declaration of victory.

Une perm' a Paris…Have a Coca-Cola
(PARIS LEAVE)

…*Yank friendliness comes to the Eiffel Tower*

It's a natural impulse for a Yank soldier to share his home ways and home things with friendly foreigners abroad. The invitation *Have a Coke* is a symbol of his feeling of friendliness toward folks in Paris. It says *We're your allies—we wish you well* in a way as American as baseball or the corner drugstore at home. Wherever you hear *Have a Coke* you hear the voice of America…inviting you to enjoy *the pause that refreshes,*—a national custom now becoming an international symbol of good will as well.

* * *

Our fighting men meet up with Coca-Cola many places overseas, where it's bottled on the spot. Coca-Cola has been a globe-trotter "since way back when".

Coca-Cola
-the global
high-sign

You naturally hear Coca-Cola called by its friendly abbreviation "Coke". Both mean the quality product of The Coca-Cola Company

COPYRIGHT 1945, THE COCA-COLA COMPANY

YANKS CLEAR GREENLAND OF NAZIS

In an effort to break up the establishment of Nazi bases in the far north, Coast Guardsmen blast their way through ice floes off Greenland.

An intense hunt goes on for two months for a hidden radio and weather station used to transmit vital information to German planes and bases.

Hidden in icy caves, scientific equipment is captured along with the crew of the Nazi weather station.

Captured German trawler crew is taken to U.S. cutter Northland.

The Americans bring the German trawler to Boston. Boarded before the German crew had time to set off demolition charges, the ship is complete in every detail, including rocket launchers and 37mm guns. This vital mid-Atlantic base is now secure.

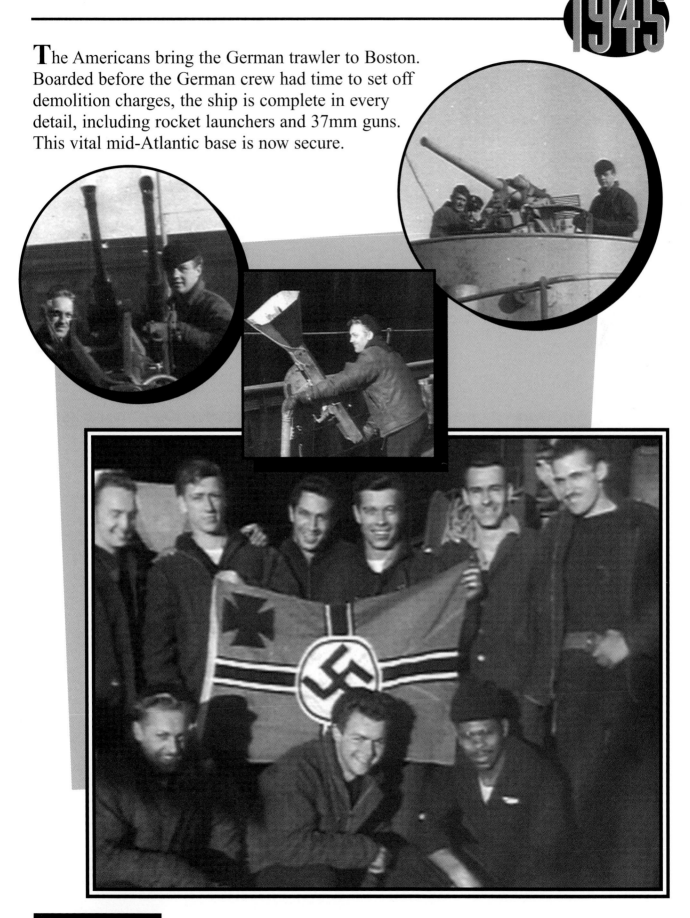

Nazi **TERROR** **IN** **WARSAW**

These smuggled pictures, taken by the Underground in August 1944, are the first scenes to be shown of the Warsaw uprising. Germans bomb and shell sections held by the Poles, moving in tanks and heavy equipment.

The Germans systematically reduce the Warsaw ghetto to rubble, exterminating thousands.

The Germans take over all parts of Warsaw.

After a bloody two-month battle, the Poles capitulate and sign an armistice with the Nazis.

Starving Poles strip dead horses for food.

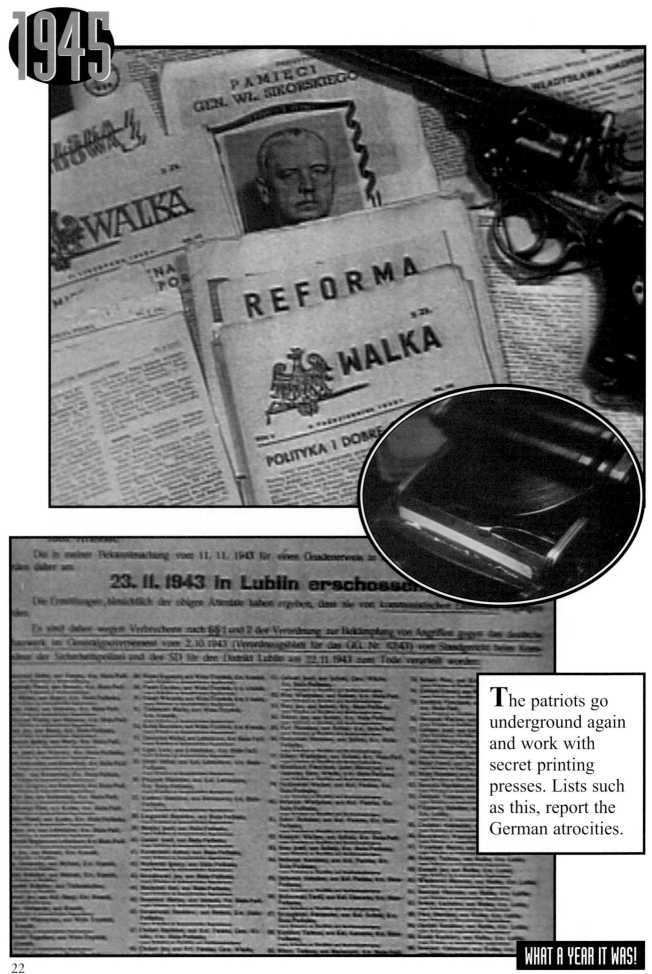

23. II. 1943 in Lublin erschossen

The patriots go underground again and work with secret printing presses. Lists such as this, report the German atrocities.

The Underground continues to cover public places with symbols of resistance and every day sees new acts of sabotage, resulting in only two-thirds of Nazi troops and supplies reaching their destinations.

The Poles string up caricatures of Hitler.

1945

13 NATIONS DECLARE WAR AGAINST GERMANY

DAILY ... CIRCULATION

ARGENTINA, CHILE, EGYPT, ECUADOR, FINLAND, LEBANON, PARAGUAY, PERU, SAUDI ARABIA, SYRIA, TURKEY, URUGUAY, VENEZUELA

We had 5 days for our Honeymoon

Our first day—we found the loveliest honeymoon place. "Loveliest to remember—" you said, "the darling softness of your hands." (Oh, thanks for Jergens Lotion. Jergens furnishes softness-protection most hand skin needs.)

Poetry in the afternoons. "'Your soft hand is a woman of itself'," you read. "That's true, darling," you said—and kissed my fingers. (Oh, poor girls, who let their hands get rough—when Jergens Lotion hand care is so easy!)

Lovely New York Models use Jergens Lotion, nearly 5 to 1. Are sure of softer, adorable hands, using Jergens; wise *protection* against roughness. Like professional hand care. Two ingredients in Jergens are so right for helping even harsh skin to longed-for smoothness that many doctors prescribe them. No stickiness. 10¢ to $1.00, plus tax.

for the softest, adorable Hands, USE

JERGENS LOTION

WAC MEDICAL UNITS NEEDED

For your country's sake today—

For your own sake tomorrow

GO TO THE NEAREST RECRUITING STATION
OF THE ARMED SERVICE OF YOUR CHOICE

Surgeon General Kirk, shown here with Colonel Hobby, head of the WACs, sends out an urgent appeal for 8,000 more WACs to assist nurses in the 60 general hospitals in the United States.

WESTERN UNION

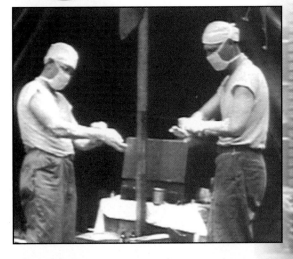

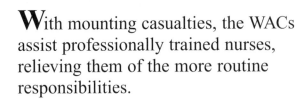

With mounting casualties, the WACs assist professionally trained nurses, relieving them of the more routine responsibilities.

The nurses care for as many as 40 sick and wounded soldiers instead of the normal 10. The WACs serve as medical and surgical technicians, assisting in the operating rooms, x-ray labs and drug dispensaries.

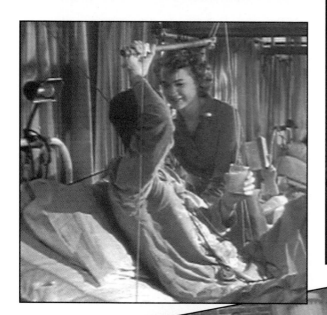

The WACs, working side by side with civilian doctors and nurses, take deep pride in caring for our wounded soldiers and restoring them to health.

WHAT A YEAR IT WAS!

HOSPITAL CORPS WAVES

Navy's Women Help to Keep "As Many Men at as Many Guns as Many Days as Possible"

In the occupational therapy ward, Marilyn Kohlenberg, PhM 3/c, teaches the fine art of fly-tying. She has released a man for duty overseas—has been trained in an important wartime profession that offers women a bright post-war future. Although no WAVE can be guaranteed assignment to any particular department or section of the Navy, half of this year's quota of 20,000 WAVES will be assigned to the Hospital Corps after completing basic training.

A hydro-therapy specialist, Pharmacist's Mate 2/c Blanche Brotzman is shown giving a fracture treatment at the United States Naval Hospital, St. Albans, New York. 10,000 more WAVES Corpsmen like her are needed immediately to serve in wards, laboratories, and records departments of Naval hospitals and other Medical Department facilities in the U. S.

Preparing sterile equipment for an operation. Zelma Shelley, PhM 2/c, had no previous experience in medical work before enlisting. *Any* American woman between 20 and 36, with two years of high school, no children under 18 years, and in normal good health, is eligible for enlistment in the WAVES.

SERVE IN THE NAVY

JOIN THE

WAVES

OFFICIAL PHOTOS, U.S. NAVY

Put yourself in the picture! If *you* want to fill a man's job and still do a woman's work, talk it over with the nearest Navy Recruiting Office immediately. Or write WAVES, Washington 25, D. C., for the free booklet, "The Story of You in Navy Blue."

THIS MESSAGE CONTRIBUTED BY THE MAKERS OF

PEPPERELL SHEETS

Dry Scalp is nature's call for help...

5 drops a day / check Dry Scalp

help nature give you good-looking hair!

YOUR HAIR CAN TALK! Loose dandruff, and lifeless-looking, hard-to-comb hair is Nature's way of saying you have Dry Scalp . . . that natural scalp oils need help. Give Nature that help. Supplement natural scalp oils with five drops of 'Vaseline' Hair Tonic daily. Always use as a massage before shampooing, too. You *see* and *feel* the difference. Your hair gets that natural, "just-combed" look. Your scalp feels better. Be sure to get 'Vaseline' Hair Tonic, the hair tonic that contains no alcohol or other drying ingredients.

Vaseline
REG. U. S. PAT. OFF.
HAIR TONIC
double care... both scalp and hair

CHINESE PEOPLE IN FLIGHT

Thousands of refugees from the Chinese cities of Hengyang and Guilin flee the Japanese.

The refugees pause only to eat and rest briefly.

Oil "Know-how" that Answered Combat Problems_

CAN HELP SOLVE SPRINGTIME CAR PROBLEMS FOR YOU!

Protect Your Car the Quality Way— Change to Summer Mobiloil

IN SWELTERING HEAT, under grueling combat strain, U.S. Army equipment stands up magnificently because our Army experts do a magnificent job of regular, scientific servicing.

What better lesson for U.S. motorists . . . whose older cars need Complete Summer Servicing right now!

Get complete Mobilubrication today!

Your Mobilgas dealer uses Mobiloil and Mobilgreases from the same refineries which have supplied millions of barrels of fine petroleum products to the Armed Forces . . . applies them scientifically, following a chart of your make of car.

Engine, radiator, gears, chassis are thoroughly protected...and with this service goes a careful gas-saving check-up of spark plugs, air cleaner and other important car parts. Older cars need better care. *Get it* at Mobilgas dealers!

SOCONY VACUUM OIL COMPANY, INC. and Affiliates: Magnolia Petroleum Company, General Petroleum Corp. of California.

Official U.S. Navy Photo

Tune in
"INFORMATION PLEASE"
Sponsored by your Mobilgas Dealer
Monday Evenings, 9:30 E.W.T.—NBC

FOR QUALITY PROTECTION_ Mobiloil

Mobilgas SOCONY-VACUUM

Mobiloil

_And Complete Mobilubrication

General Krueger, commanding the 6th Army, directs the campaign that gives the Japanese troops a major setback and moves our men closer to the Philippine capital.

YANKS CLOSE IN ON MANILA

LST's, amphibious landing craft, hit the beach loaded with tanks and supplies.

WHAT A YEAR IT WAS!

As American troops head north through the town of San Fabian, Filipinos give our boys a big welcome and General Griswold is decorated in the traditional island fashion.

One of the fiercest battles of the campaign occurs near Baguio, where heavy Allied casualties are sustained.

A marker commemorates a Japanese captain who boasted he would capture Bataan in one week. He later committed hara-kiri.

The new five star general of the Army, Douglas MacArthur, arrives to receive his well-earned laurels.

With the invasion of Japan imminent, MacArthur receives a hero's welcome.

MANILA LIBERATED AFTER THREE YEARS OF JAPANESE OCCUPATION

MANILA

Japanese demolition squads systematically destroy everything in their path as they retreat before the American advance. No portion of the city escapes destruction.

At Rizal Stadium, American tanks advance to clean out Japanese snipers hidden in the bleachers and under the stadium.

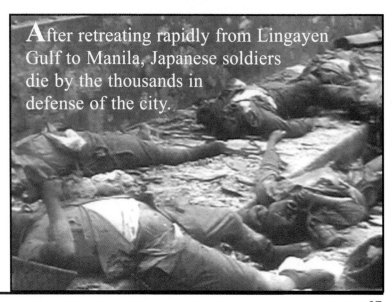

After retreating rapidly from Lingayen Gulf to Manila, Japanese soldiers die by the thousands in defense of the city.

The attack on southern Manila commences with assault boats. Under heavy Japanese fire, the final phase of the city's capture is underway. Hiding out in sniper's nests, the enemy puts up tremendous resistance.

Flame throwers destroy snipers.

Big guns bombard the Intramuros section, where the Japanese make a last stand. The fighting is over in Manila.

WHAT A YEAR IT WAS!

MARINES TAKE IWO JIMA AFTER BLOODIEST BATTLE IN HISTORY

Joe Rosenthal's photo of the second flag raising on Mt. Suribachi, one of the most recognized photos of World War II.

Despite over two months of constant bombing of Iwo Jima, a strategically located island in the North Pacific, when 30,000 U.S. Marines land they find the Japanese hidden in caves, tunnels and bombproof underground bunkers. Thousands of Marines are killed by these unseen Japanese. Finally, the Marines capture the airfields and raise the American flag atop the island's volcanic mountain.

When the struggle for the island is over 26 days later, the fiercest battle in America's history results in 22,099 casualties, including dead, wounded and missing in action. Nearly all 21,000 Japanese soldiers are dead.

YANK SHELLS HIT KEHL IN RHINELAND

From Strasbourg, Nazi positions across the Rhine are shelled. Despite strong Nazi resistance, Strasbourg is taken and Kehl comes within range of American guns. Pillboxes are smashed and a factory is blasted.

WHAT A YEAR IT WAS!

un_and *WHOOSH!*

From Sensational Socony-Vacuum Super Fuel Developments—Deadly New Speed, Power, Fighting Punch for U. S. Warplanes!

That's *FLYING HORSEPOWER!*

War Power Today—Car Power Tomorrow! After Victory, You'll Get Flying Horsepower!

ALL the gasoline power your car's engine will take!...that's what you can expect of *New Mobilgas* after Victory!... FLYING HORSEPOWER!

For your post-war Mobilgas will contain the same super fuel ingredients now powering fighters to faster take-offs, climbs and speeds...now giving bombers greater striking power on longer runs. That's Flying Horsepower in the air!

And here's what it will mean to cars tomorrow:

Flashing take-offs in traffic, new power-

pull on hills, instant throttle response at any speed, under every driving condition!

This is Socony-Vacuum's promise to motorists, backed by 12 years' pioneering in super fuels, by the World's Greatest Catalytic Cracking Program, a $90,000,-000 investment in the future.

Look forward to the New Mobilgas...to Flying Horsepower in your car. You'll give 'er the gun—and *whoosh!*

SOCONY-VACUUM OIL COMPANY, INC. and Affiliates: Magnolia Petroleum Company, General Petroleum Corporation of California

Navy Photo

bilgas AND Mobiloil

FILIPINO CIVILIANS LIBERATED

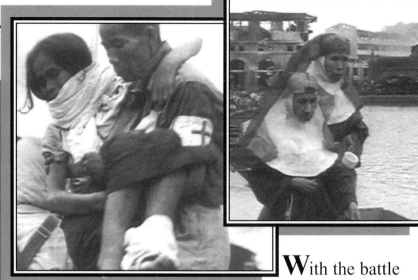

With the battle over, the Pasig River is bridged by the Yanks. The Philippine capital is free of Japanese occupation and civilians, forced to stay within Intramuros to shield Japanese soldiers from Yank artillery fire, are rescued.

General Douglas MacArthur returns to inspect the damage.

On reconquered Corregidor, where the infamous March of Death began, General MacArthur delivers a command that insures the future liberty of the Philippines. *"I see that the old flag staff still stands. Have your troops hoist the colors to its peak and let no enemy ever haul them down."*

WHAT A YEAR IT WAS!

1945 ADVERTISEMENT

45

ROOSEVELT DIES ON EVE OF WAR VICTORY

Two Parts ★★★ FRIDAY MORNING, APRIL 13, 1945 DAILY, FIVE CENTS

APRIL 12 — A stunned nation learned of the death of its 32nd president, Franklin Delano Roosevelt, a man characterized by Senator Robert A. Taft as "the greatest figure of our time." Roosevelt's presidency was marked by initiating the New Deal, a federal program designed to rescue the nation from its deep economic depression. FDR was the only president elected to serve four terms and the first president to introduce "fireside chats." His death came at a time of victories for the armies and fleets under his command.

Hours before his death, Roosevelt complained of a bad headache, which was followed by a cerebral hemorrhage. Vice President Harry S. Truman was sworn in as president less than two hours later.

Mourners gather to pay a tearful farewell to their beloved president. The loss of Franklin Delano Roosevelt is deeply felt by people around the world.

1945

"The greatest champion of freedom who has ever brought help and comfort from the new world to the old."

— *Winston Churchill, from the eulogy in St. Paul's Cathedral*

In the cabinet room of the White House, a somber Harry S. Truman is sworn in as President.

WHAT A YEAR IT WAS!

April 28:
The dictatorship of Benito Mussolini, "Father of Italian Fascism," came to an ugly end as "Il Duce" was riddled with bullets by partisan Italians.

MUSSOLINI EXECUTED BY PARTISAN ITALIANS

Mussolini's corpse is brought to Milan, where he and his mistress are hanged by their heels in a public square.

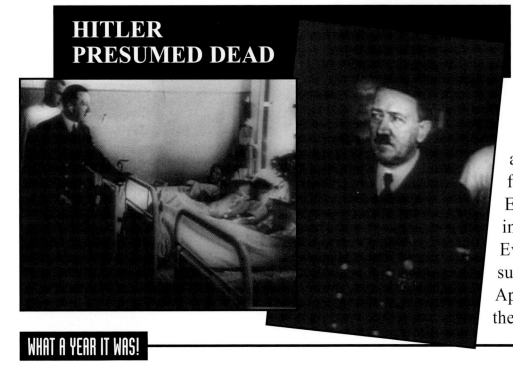

HITLER PRESUMED DEAD

Adolf Hitler, who survived a bomb planted by one of his own officers in 1944, was presumably alive until the fall of Berlin. Evidence seems to indicate that he and Eva Braun committed suicide in a bunker on April 30, the day after their marriage.

"I'll be Home for Christmas!"

Crowd in closer little fellow—your daddy's home! This is the brightest Christmas in your lifetime—with the black shadow of war lifted from all our hearts, millions of our men rolling home, lining the rails of every ship afloat, and framed in the windows of every bus, ashore!

After four years of asking people *not* to travel, it's a heartwarming task for Greyhound to speed the reunion of fighting men with their loved ones—and freely to carry all the other millions of Americans who want and need to travel by bus on Year-End trips, on business, on winter vacations.

Yes, there'll be days (especially around Christmas) when buses in many areas will be crowded. People who can arrange their trips just before or just after these busy periods are wise. But, today, Greyhound is not only able to offer travel without the old taboos, but schedules are more frequent than ever before—trips are faster—more seats are available—Express service is back—carefree Expense-Paid Tours are yours again.

And, from here in, we invite you to watch for further bus improvements and innovations. *They're coming fast, and Greyhound will again lead the way.*

GREYHOUND

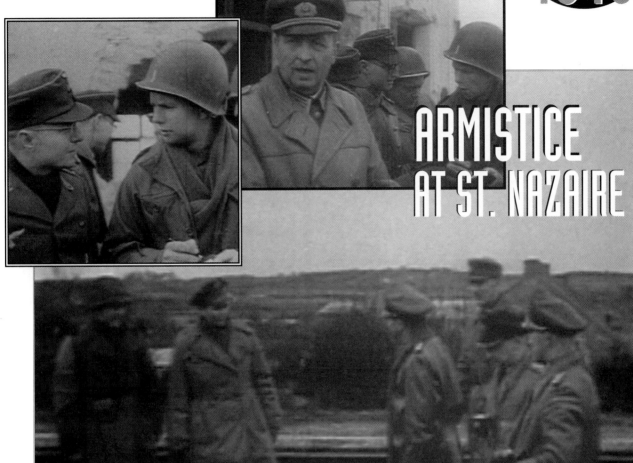

ARMISTICE AT ST. NAZAIRE

Members of the German garrison meet Americans at St. Nazaire to discuss terms of a three-hour truce under which French civilians may be evacuated.

Flying the international flag of mercy, a train prepares to transport refugees.

Smiling soldiers stand by as these victims of war board the train to be reunited with family and friends.

GERMANY SIGNS UNCONDITIONAL SURRENDER

MAY 7: The war in Europe came to an end today as Germany capitulated to Allied demands. For the first time in five years, eight months and six days the battlefields lay silent.

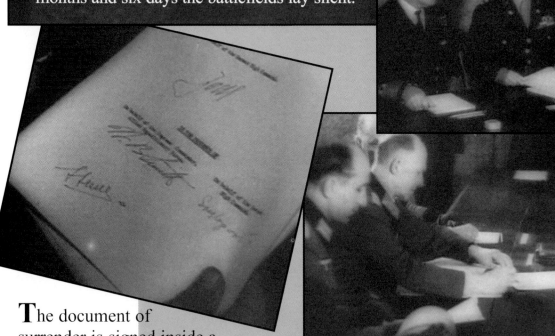

The document of surrender is signed inside a little schoolhouse at Rheims with representatives from the United States, France, Great Britain and the U.S.S.R. present. General Alfred Jodl, Nazi Chief of Staff, signs the document formally ending all German resistance. Lt. General Walter Bedell Smith signs for the Supreme Command.

The success of one of history's most massive and most brilliant campaigns brings a moment of well-earned joy to an American soldier named Ike Eisenhower.

XTRA! 9 A.M. FINAL

MONDAY MORNING, MAY 7, 1945

DAILY, FIVE CENTS

V-E DAY!

What God Hath Wrought

Nazis Surrender Unconditionally to Allied Powers

REIMS (France) May 7 (A.P.)—Germany surrendered unconditionally to the western Allies and Russia at 2:41 a.m. French time today.

The surrender took place at a little red school house which is the headquarters of Gen. Eisenhower.

The surrender which brought the war in Europe to a formal end after five years, eight months and six days of bloodshed and destruction was signed for Germany by Col. Gen. Gustav Jodl. (Jodl is the new chief of staff of the German army.)

It was signed for the supreme Allied command by Lt. Gen. Walter Bedell Smith, chief of staff for Gen. Eisenhower.

It was also signed by Gen. Ivan Susloparoff for Russia and by Gen. Francois Sevez for France.

(A sour note came from the German-controlled radio at Prague. A broadcast monitored by the Czechoslovak government offices in London said the German commander in Czechoslovakia did not recognize the surrender of Adm. Doenitz and would fight on until his forces "have secured free passage for German troops out of the country.")

LONDON, May 7. (AP) — German broadcasts today said "all fighting German troops" had surrendered unconditionally, and the world waited for an official Allied announcement expected from the Big Three capitals.

BULLETINS ON SURRENDER

LONDON, May 7. (AP) — Adm. Karl Doenitz has "ordered

Although the nation is grieving the recent death of President Roosevelt and the war in the Pacific rages on, the end of the war with Germany is met with great jubilance in the United States.

May 23: One of the most despicable chapters in history comes to a close as the Third Reich collapses and leaders of the movement are arrested. Among those arrested by Allied troops are Grand Marshal Karl Doenitz, leader of the new rump government, and Albert Speer, Minister of Economics and Production. Heinrich Himmler, treacherous architect of the concentration camps, commits suicide on his arrest.

BATTLE TO THE DEATH ON OKINAWA

On Easter Sunday, U.S. forces assault Okinawa, a 62-mile island containing airfields and naval bases valuable to our Pacific strategy. Unrelenting bombardment from the offshore fleet precedes the assault landing craft.

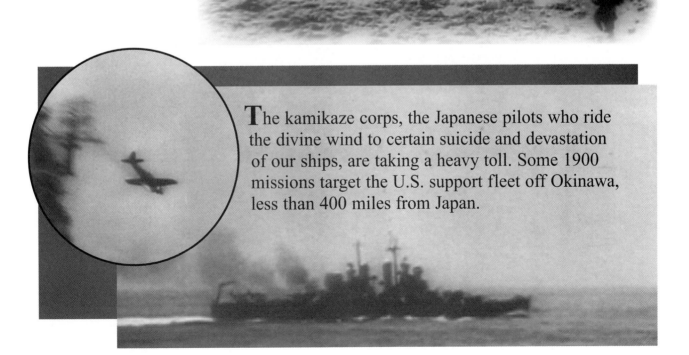

The kamikaze corps, the Japanese pilots who ride the divine wind to certain suicide and devastation of our ships, are taking a heavy toll. Some 1900 missions target the U.S. support fleet off Okinawa, less than 400 miles from Japan.

Tank flame throwers blast enemy caves on strategic Sawtooth Ridge. Newsreel, Signal Corps and Marine cameramen risk their lives to record the action near Sugarloaf Mt. and Chocolate Drop Hill.

After a
four-month
battle that
took
110,000
Japanese
lives and
12,500
American lives, the bloody
battle for Okinawa ends in victory for
the U.S. forces.

The Japanese could not afford to lose Okinawa, as it brings the Americans to the gates of Tokyo, the next big step toward victory over Japan.

Bonds by the Billions

The War Bonds you HOLD are FIGHTING BONDS

The Seventh War Loan—the Mighty Seventh—is giving every red-blooded American his opportunity to put his dollars into the Victory March against tyranny. Pour out your might for the Mighty Seventh.

The 5-Star leaders of our fighting men—Marshall, Leahy, MacArthur, King, Eisenhower, Nimitz, Arnold—say to you:

"We, upon whom has been placed the responsibility of leading the American Forces, appeal to you with all possible earnestness to invest in War Bonds to the fullest extent of your capacity" ★ ★ ★ ★ ★

These 5-Star leaders ask you to buy war bonds and hold them.

And, remember, the war bonds you *hold* are the *fighting* bonds.

And they're the best and safest investment in the world. So, save for your country—save for yourself.

★ ★ ★ ★ ★

BONDS BY THE BILLIONS BY BRINK'S—

Brink's, the World's Largest Money Movers, haul war bonds by the billions, as well as dollars. Over 125 billions in 1944. Brink's operate more than six hundred armored trucks more than seven million miles a year. In the past twenty-five years Brink's have bought more than 1600 Internationals, and during that time 90% of Brink's trucks have been International Trucks.

INTERNATIONAL HARVESTER

BUY BONDS

LIBERTY FLEET

Buy WAR BONDS

INTERNATIONAL Trucks

PRESIDENT TRUMAN WARNS JAPAN OF IMPENDING DESTRUCTION

> **" ...only surrender can prevent the kind of ruin which they have seen come to Germany... "**

"There can be no peace in the world until the military power of Japan is destroyed, with the same completeness as was the European dictators. To do that, we are now engaged in a process of deploying millions of our armed forces against Japan in a mass movement of troops and supplies and weapons over fourteen thousand miles – a military and naval feat unequaled in all history.

"Substantial portions of Japan's key industrial centers have been leveled to the ground in a series of record incendiary raids. What has already happened to Tokyo will happen to every Japanese city whose industries feed the Japanese war machine. If the Japanese insist on continuing resistance beyond the point of reason, their country will suffer the same destruction as Germany. Our blows will destroy their whole modern industrial plan and organization which they have built up during the past century and which they are now devoting to a hopeless cause.

"We have no desire or intention to destroy or enslave the Japanese people. But only surrender can prevent the kind of ruin which they have seen come to Germany as a result of continued, useless resistance."

WHAT A YEAR IT WAS!

AMERICA UNLEASHES THE ATOMIC BOMB

The first atomic weapon to be used in war is dropped on Hiroshima at 9:15 a.m. on Monday, August 6 by a B-29 Superfortress piloted by Colonel Paul W. Tibbetts, Jr. named Enola Gay (the pilot's mother's name). The bomb, named "Little Boy," has the power of 20,000 tons of TNT.

On August 9, another B-29 Superfortress piloted by Major Charles W. Sweeney drops a second A-bomb, "Fat Man," on the city of Nagasaki.

The total toll: 70,000 dead, 120,000 wounded, 290,000 homeless.

For security reasons details are kept secret by the U.S. government. However, it is disclosed that the atomic bomb achieves its awesome power by harnessing atomic fission — the splitting of atoms.

ATOMIC BOMB ATTACKS ON HIROSHIMA AND NAGASAKI FORCE JAPAN'S SURRENDER

On Sunday, September 2, 1945, aboard the U.S.S. Missouri in Tokyo Bay, the most horrible war in history comes to its complete and formal end and V-J Day is officially recognized.

WHAT A YEAR IT WAS!

INSTRUMENT OF SURRENDER

W e, acting by command of and in behalf of the Emperor of Japan, the Japanese Government and the Japanese Imperial General Headquarters, hereby accept the provisions set forth in the declaration issued by the heads of the Governments of the United States, China and Great Britain on 26 July 1945 at Potsdam, and subsequently adhered to by the Union of Soviet Socialist Republics, which four powers are hereafter referred to as the Allied Powers.

We hereby proclaim the unconditional surrender to the Allied Powers of the Japanese Imperial General Headquarters and of all Japanese armed forces and all armed forces under Japanese control wherever situated.

We hereby command all Japanese forces wherever situated and the Japanese people to cease hostilities forthwith, to preserve and save from damage all ships, aircraft, and military and civil property and to comply with all requirements which may be imposed by the Supreme Commander for the Allied Powers or by agencies of the Japanese Government at his direction.

We hereby command the Japanese Imperial General Headquarters to issue at once orders to the Commanders of all Japanese forces and all forces under Japanese control wherever situated to surrender unconditionally themselves and all forces under their control.

We hereby command all civil, military and naval officials to obey and enforce all proclamations, orders and directives deemed by the Supreme Commander for the Allied Powers to be proper to effectuate this surrender and issued by him or under his authority and we direct all such officials to remain at their posts and to continue to perform their non-combatant duties unless specifically relieved by him or under his authority.

We hereby undertake for the Emperor, the Japanese Government and their successors to carry out the provisions of the Potsdam Declaration in good faith, and to issue whatever orders and take whatever action may be required by the Supreme Commander for the Allied Powers or by any other designated representative of the Allied Powers for the purpose of giving effect to that Declaration.

We hereby command the Japanese Imperial Government and the Japanese Imperial General Headquarters at once to liberate all allied prisoners of war and civilian internees now under Japanese control and to provide for their protection, care, maintenance and immediate transportation to places as directed.

The authority of the Emperor and the Japanese Government to rule the state shall be subject to the Supreme Commander for the Allied Powers who will take such steps as he deems proper to effectuate these terms of surrender.

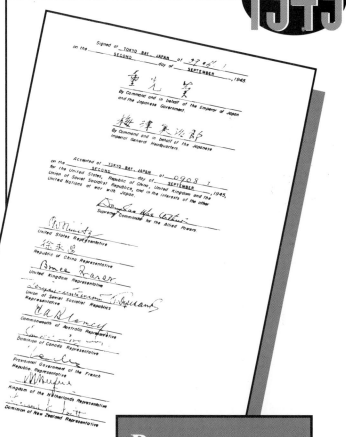

Douglas MacArthur, Supreme Commander, signs for the Allied Powers.

Prime Minister Shigemitsu signs the Instrument of Surrender for Japan.

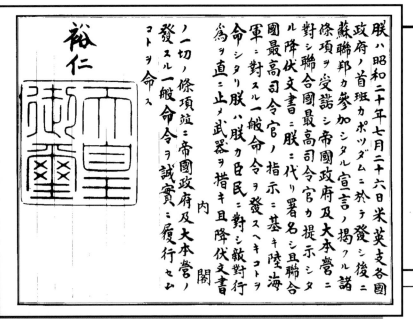

朕八昭和二十年七月二十六日米英支各國政府ノ首班カポツダムニ於テ發シ後ニ蘇聯邦カ參加シタル宣言ノ揭クル諸條項ヲ受諾シ帝國政府及大本營ニ對シ聯合國最高司令官ヲ提示シタル降伏文書ニ朕ニ代リ署名シ且聯合國最高司令官ノ指示ニ基キ陸海軍ニ對スル一般命令ヲ發スヘキコトヲ命シタリ朕ハ朕カ臣民ニ對シ敵對行為ヲ直ニ止メ武器ヲ措キ且降伏文書ノ一切ノ條項竝ニ帝國政府及大本營ノ發スル一般命令ヲ誠實ニ履行セム

裕仁

内閣

昭和二十年九月二日

内閣總理大臣公爵　稔彥王

國務大臣　近衞文麿

内務大臣　山崎巖

司法大臣

大藏大臣　津島壽一

運輸大臣　小日山直登

外務大臣　重光葵

海軍大臣　米内光政

團農林大臣

文部大臣

厚生大臣

商工大臣

陸軍大臣

General Hsu Yung-Chang
signs for China.

NAZI GERMANY'S LEADERS ON TRIAL AT NUREMBERG FOR WAR CRIMES

NO LOITERING
Das Herumstehen
Ist Verboten

The Palace of Justice in Nuremberg, Germany, is the setting for this historic trial of Nazi war criminals.

For the first time in history, war leaders are being tried by an international court. Representatives of the United States, Great Britain, Russia and France sit in judgment.

Earphones provide multi-lingual translations enabling judges, lawyers, defendants and spectators to follow the trial in German, French, Russian or English.

Defendants Hermann Goering, Rudolph Hess, Joachim von Ribbentrop, Alfred Rosenberg, Hans Fritsche—names that struck terror into the hearts of so many—along with 17 others, are on trial for planning world conquest and the death and enslavement of millions.

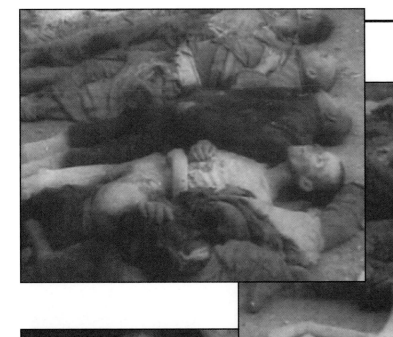

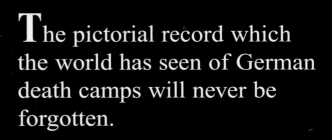

The pictorial record which the world has seen of German death camps will never be forgotten.

The defendants all plead not guilty, but the Nuremberg criminals are held accountable.

United States Supreme Court Justice Robert H. Jackson opens the prosecution's case with the following remarks:

"The privilege of opening the first trial in history for crimes against the peace of the world imposes a grave responsibility. The wrongs which we seek to condemn and punish have been so calculated, so malignant and so devastating that civilization cannot tolerate their being ignored because it cannot survive their being repeated."

TIMELINE (NON-WAR EVENTS)

JUN 30 President Truman terminates National Office of Civilian Defense	**DEC 19** President Truman nominates Eleanor Roosevelt as U.S. delegate to the United Nations
OCT 11 Tax reduction approved by House of Representatives 343-10	**DEC 22** Marshal Tito gains recognition of his Yugoslav government by U.S. and Great Britain
NOV 6 William O'Dwyer elected mayor of New York City	
NOV 16 Drs. Robert J. Oppenheimer, Irving Langmuir and Arthur H. Compton issue warning that an atomic war could render the world uninhabitable	Formosa (Taiwan) returned to Chinese sovereignty
NOV 19 President Truman asks Congress to act on legislation granting compulsory health insurance	Alaska becomes first U.S. territory or state to enact an anti-discrimination law
DEC 17 U.S. Senate unanimously adopts resolution urging aid in establishment of Jewish commonwealth in Palestine	U.S. boasts world's most powerful naval air force

UNITED NATIONS IS BORN

JUNE
26

Delegates from 30 nations approve the historic charter establishing the United Nations at a meeting in San Francisco.

President Truman greets a cheering crowd in attendance at the War Memorial Opera House. "Oh, what a great day this can be in history." He declares that the world must now use the new "instrument of peace" or "...we shall betray all those who have died in order that we might meet here in freedom to create it..."

U.S. Senate ratifies U.N. Charter 89-2 on July 28.

POTSDAM CONFERENCE FAILS MISERABLY

JULY
26

The conference at Potsdam fails to reduce tensions between Russia and the Western Allies. Without the presence of the late President Roosevelt and Winston Churchill, who returned to England for elections, the irreconcilable differences seem more insurmountable than before.

Stalin won't budge from his position on Poland and free elections in Bulgaria, Hungary and Rumania.

The leaders are in agreement on sending an ultimatum to Japan demanding its immediate surrender or suffer severe consequences.

OCTOBER
20

In their struggle for the Holy Land, Egypt, Lebanon, Iraq and Syria join forces, warning that a Jewish state in Palestine will result in war.

ARAB STATES UNITE TO FORM ARAB LEAGUE

PEOPLE

NEW FRENCH ENVOY TO U.S.

The French embassy in Washington is now home to Monsieur Henri Bonnet, first accredited ambassador from the traditional French government, and his wife, Madame Bonnet.

Monsieur Bonnet is the former Minister of Information in the de Gaulle government.

The new commander of the American armed forces in China, Major General Wedemeyer, arrives on a three-day inspection tour.

With the Ledo-Burma Road clear of the Japanese army, General Wedemeyer's troops are ready to move forward.

WHAT A YEAR IT WAS!

1945

LET THEM DRINK JUICE

Unhappy about liberated Europeans offering U.S. soldiers jugs of wine, Dr. Ella Alexander Boole makes a pitch for the healthier choice of fruit juice.

September: Los Angeles born Tokyo Rose (Iva Togori) is arrested in Yokohama and will stand trial in America for treason stemming from her seductive appeals to American G.I.'s stationed in the South Pacific to surrender.

Marlene Dietrich Returns From 11-Month USO Tour

Major General Patrick J. Hurley presents to Chiang Kai-shek his credentials as Ambassador Plenipotentiary to the national government of the Republic of China.

30,000 to 40,000 Allied Powers photographers cover the war and record events.

WHAT A YEAR IT WAS!

Boeing Stratocruiser (above) and Boeing B-29 Superfortress

Trail-blazer for peacetime flight

The Boeing B-29 Superfortress is something more than the weapon that helped win the war against Japan. It embodies principles that will *revolutionize air transport* now that victory is won.

Not only have the great Boeing planes in which you may soon travel already been designed . . . a military version of the first true super-transport of the future—the Boeing Stratocruiser—has broken all records for transcontinental flight, with a coast-to-coast average speed of 383 miles per hour!

To meet the necessities of long-range global war, Boeing made the *four-engine* airplane our most potent aerial weapon and demonstrated its great commercial future. Boeing has had more experience

in the design and building of four-engine aircraft than any other manufacturer in the world. Like the Superfortress, the new Stratocruiser has four engines —and even greater horsepower will be added.

Like the B-29, this super-transport has the extraordinarily efficient Boeing wing, giving it *huge carrying capacity—plus* higher performance and greater economy in operation than any other transport.

Again, like the Boeing Superfortress, the Stratocruiser benefits from Boeing's long leadership in stratosphere research and the production of aircraft for *high-level, over-weather operation*. It has improved pressurized cabins—*plus* new refinements in sound-proofing and air-conditioning.

It has all the structural and aerodynamic advances of the last three years, proved in war on Boeing-built aircraft—all the new features contributing to safe navigation, ease of control and dependable performance—*plus* passenger comfort never before imagined. The Boeing Stratocruiser expresses, as no other commercial airplane has yet done, man's growing understanding of the laws of flight.

• • •

Now that peace is here, Boeing principles of research, design, engineering and manufacture will bring you the Stratocruiser and other advances in air transport . . . and you may know of any airplane—if it's "Built by Boeing" it's built to lead.

DESIGNERS OF THE B-29 SUPERFORTRESS • THE FLYING FORTRESS • THE NEW STRATOCRUISER **BOEING**
THE KAYDET TRAINER • THE STRATOLINER • PAN AMERICAN CLIPPERS

THE BIG THREE GATHER AT YALTA FOR HISTORIC MEETING

Franklin D. Roosevelt confers with Joseph Stalin and Winston Churchill in Yalta to map out final steps to crush the Axis and establish peace. Discussions include the division of post-war Europe into zones of political influence as well as expediting the war against Japan. It is the last meeting of the original "Big Three" as FDR, already tired and looking strained, dies only two months later.

WHAT A YEAR IT WAS!

DEWEY WANTS ACTIVE PEACE ROLE FOR U.S.

In a speech delivered to a Lincoln Day dinner of the Republican party, New York's Governor Thomas E. Dewey emphasized the role of the U.S. as leader in any international peace plans. He also praised the success of the U.S. capitalistic system as being responsible for enormous initiative and inventive genius. Dewey closed by saying, "The very heart of that system is the classic liberal concept that every man is his own master and that government exists to keep men free."

SECRETARY OF STATE EDWARD R. STETTINIUS ISSUES PLEA FOR HUMAN RIGHTS

"The four freedoms stated by President Roosevelt — freedom of speech, freedom of religion, freedom from want and freedom from fear — are from the point of view of the United States, the fundamental freedoms which encompass all other rights and freedoms. The United States government will work actively and tirelessly, both for its own people and through the international organization for peoples generally, toward the protection and the promotion of these rights and freedoms."

Sgt. Sabu ("Elephant Boy") is awarded the Distinguished Flying Cross for riding a U.S. bomber as a tail gunner in an attack on a Japanese convoy.

1945 ADVERTISEMENT

1. **Today**—Army Air Force pilots are snugly protected against stratosphere cold in "electrically-warm" G-E Flying suits—cousins to the G-E Blanket, and made in the same factory.

2. **Postwar with the G-E Blanket.** Maybe, say at 10 o'clock some cool night, you'll turn on the G-E Blanket a few minutes before you're ready to go to bed. Then climb in between smooth, "sunshiny-warm" sheets.

3. **At midnight:** Weather gets bitter, bed stays warm. The G-E Blanket will control bed-warmth just the way your furnace thermostat controls house-warmth.

4. **At 2:00 a. m.:** Can take the place of three blankets. The G-E Blanket weighs only 5¾ lbs. (Three ordinary blankets would weigh around 15 lbs.) Yet it's always as warm as *you* want it!

5. **At 7:00 a. m.:** Wake up wonderfully refreshed. No crushing blanket-weight, no cramped positions because of a chilly bed—under a G-E Blanket. Just heavenly, night-long "baby" sleep.

For a New Kind of Sleeping Comfort Tomorrow:

 Automatic Blankets

GENERAL ELECTRIC

NEW AUTOMATIC BLANKET WILL ENABLE YOU TO SLEEP COZILY IN ANY WEATHER

AFTER THE WAR, many Americans will welcome the new "electrically-warm" Automatic Blanket as one of the most wonderful of all new comforts.

▶ Made by the General Electric Company, the G-E Blanket will do what no other blanket—or any human being—has ever successfully managed to do: it will flood beds with even, restful, sunshiny warmth all night long.

▶ Almost as light as a single regular blanket, the G-E Blanket can *do the job of three*. Even in zero weather,

"cold-blooded" Americans will be able to wear summer-weight night clothes, keep windows wide open—and be perfectly comfortable.

▶ The G-E Blanket plugs in just like a lamp. A Bedside Control regulates bed temperature to the user's will, adjusts *automatically* to any normal weather change.

▶ Thousands of American homes are already outfitted with G.E.'s lightweight, easy-to-care-for Blankets, which will be available in a variety of pastel

shades. Approved by the Underwriters' Laboratories, Inc.

▶ For further information write: The General Electric Co., Dept. L55, Bridgeport, Conn.

TUNE IN: "*The G-E House Party,*" *every afternoon, Monday thru Friday, 4 p. m., E.W.T., CBS.* "*The G-E All-Girl Orchestra,*" *Sunday, 10 p. m., E.W.T., NBC.* "*The World Today,*" *News, Monday thru Friday, 6:45 p. m., E.W.T., CBS.*

FOR VICTORY ... BUY WAR BONDS NOW

BRITAIN HONORS ITS HOME GUARD

The King of England and the Royal Family, along with thousands of Londoners, gather in Hyde Park to pay tribute to Britain's Home Guard.

These heroes patrolled roofs, watched for Nazi parachutists and undertook hundreds of home defense jobs when England's back was to the wall.

1945

HERO RETURNS

General Courtney Hodges, Georgia's foremost soldier and leader of one of America's greatest fighting teams, arrives back home after leading his victorious First Army through Germany.

One of the largest crowds in the city's history gathers to pay tribute.

Lt. Will Rogers, Jr., son of the late humorist, is promoted to first lieutenant and awarded a Bronze Star for heroism in leading a patrol during the Battle of the Bulge.

• • •

Lt. Joseph P. Kennedy, Jr. is posthumously awarded the Navy Cross for extraordinary heroism and courage.

• • •

Rear Admiral Richard Evelyn Byrd receives the Legion of Merit from FDR in White House ceremony.

NOBEL PRIZE WINNER
DECEMBER 12

The coveted Nobel Prize for Peace is awarded to Cordell Hull, former Secretary of State under President Roosevelt. Mr. Hull will be remembered as "the father of the United Nations," as it was through his efforts that the world peace organization was formed.

Dwight D. Eisenhower Becomes First American Member Of Exclusive Order Of Merit By British King

Truman Decorates Ike With Second Oak Leaf Cluster Upon Arrival In U.S.

WHAT A YEAR IT WAS!

In Tomato Juice LOOK TO LIBBY'S FOR PERFECTION

In your own tomato patch, on a golden August day, were you ever tempted to pluck a special "beauty" and suck its sun-ripe juice right then and there?

If so, your palate *knows* the true tomato goodness. The same goodness we capture and *keep* for you in our tomato juice.

Libby's, you see, is the tomato juice that's TWICE-RICH. It's rich in flavor. *And* rich in those precious "tomato vitamins", too! (An excellent source of Vitamins A and C, a ready source of Vitamins B₁ and B₂.)

We start with real "eating tomatoes" . . . grown in America's "tomato lands," picked just when their juice is rich-ripe. You'd be fascinated, we think, to follow those glorious tomatoes through the Libby kitchens, particularly if you've done some Victory canning.

You'd see them dazzling-bright under their special "shower bath"; you'd see how carefully we press out the fresh juice, how precisely we control heat. And you might find yourself a little breathless keeping up with Libby *speed*, which is a vital factor in Libby perfection.

Taste the result of all this care in our sparkling, sun-ripened juice. Always buy the tomato juice marked *Libby's*. The kind that's twice-rich. *It's perfection!*

LIBBY, McNEILL & LIBBY
CHICAGO 9, ILLINOIS

Listen to "MY TRUE STORY" . . . Thrilling, real-life dramas, every morning, Mon. through Fri. 10:00 EWT, 9:00 CWT, 11:30 MWT, 10:30 PWT. Blue Network Stations.

"WASTE" PAPER IS WAR PAPER. SAVE IT!

WHERE FOOD GROWS FINEST . . . THERE LIBBY PACKS THE BEST

Libby's
TOMATO JUICE

EMPEROR HIROHITO REPORTS DEFEAT TO HIS ANCESTORS

In keeping with Japanese religious customs, Emperor Hirohito pays a visit to the burial site of his ancestors to inform them of the Japanese defeat.

Hirohito's last visit was to report the attack on Pearl Harbor.

Priests wait as Hirohito explains the presence of American soldiers on Japanese soil.

WHAT A YEAR IT WAS!

SEPTEMBER

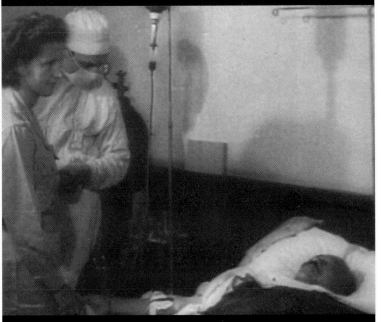

General Hideki Tojo, Premier of Japan, arrested as a war criminal along with other members of the Imperial General Staff, tries to commit suicide but is kept alive by American doctors.

NAZI COLLABORATORS EXECUTED

OCTOBER

Pierre Laval of France and Vidkun Abraham Quisling of Norway, two notorious Nazi collaborators, are put to death for aiding German occupation of their countries.

DID YOU SAY "IT'S THE END OF THE WINE?" OH — "IT'S THE END OF THE LINE!"

Stockholm newspaper Morgon-Tidningen reports Adolf Hitler developed impaired hearing resulting from last July's assassination attempt.

General Douglas MacArthur enjoyed a happy reunion with his wife, Jean, and six-year-old son, Arthur, who joined him in Manila.

Jimmy Durante Leaves On A USO Tour Overseas

1936 GOP Presidential Nominee, Alf Landon, Practices Law 37 Years After Being Admitted To The Bar

American Forces In Genoa Seize Poet Ezra Pound, Who Is Wanted For Treason

FAN-TASTIC JUSTICE

Fan dancer Sally Rand wins a California lawsuit for biting and scratching two photographers who snapped her "between fans," revealing more than a few feathers.

SWEET 16 AND NEVER BEEN... HOW MANY TIMES???

Sweet 16 Shirley Temple, filming "Kiss and Tell," was kissed 99 times by 22 actors. Was she unhappy about this? Well, she didn't give the director any lip...

Slot Machine King Frank Costello Denies Tammany Hall Influence Peddling

OUR HEARTS WERE YOUNG...ER...OLD AND GAY

Cornelia Otis Skinner complained about the overemphasis on youth in the United States and added that in France, an actress isn't worth her salt until she's 50.

THINGS THAT GO **MUMP** IN THE NIGHT

Princess Elizabeth, 18, comes down with the mumps right after her younger sister, **Princess Margaret,** recovers from them.

• • • • • • • • • • • • • • • • • •

CITY BLIGHTS

Charlie Chaplin finds himself up to his moustache in legal battles — a paternity suit filed in 1944 by Joan Berry and then a bill introduced in the U.S. Senate seeking his deportation as an undesirable alien.

Joseph Pulitzer, Jr. celebrates his 60th birthday by throwing a party and inviting over 1,100 staff members and alumni of his St. Louis Post-Dispatch.

COUPLINGS

Pvt. Red Skelton & Georgia Maureen Davis

James Dunn & Edna Rush

Congressional Medal of Honor Winner,
Cmdr. David McCampbell, No. 1 Navy Ace
(34 Enemy Planes In One Day) & Sara-Jane Heliker Kahn

Elliott Roosevelt & Faye Emerson

un COUPLINGS

Ernest Hemingway &
Martha Gellhorn

Hattie McDaniel &
James Lloyd Crawford

Barbara Hutton & Cary Grant

Carl Van Doren &
Jean Van Doren

Orson Welles' first newspaper column appears in eleven newspapers.

Hollywood's **Samuel Goldwyn** arrives in England on a special mission for the Federal Economic Administration.

Madeleine Carroll, who left Hollywood when she and her husband **Stirling Hayden** joined the war effort, gives up the screen permanently to devote herself to caring for homeless children.

Greer Garson denies she's bow-legged.

Paulette Goddard and hubby **Burgess Meredith** establish college scholarships.

THE NEW CABINET MEMBERS

Thomas C. Clark succeeds Francis Biddle as Attorney General.

Representative Clinton Anderson becomes the nation's new Secretary of Agriculture.

President Truman appoints Judge Lewis Schwellenbach as Secretary of Labor.

Charles Ross is appointed White House Press Secretary as Mrs. Ross looks on.

TRUMAN SEEKS FOOD RELIEF COUNSEL

Arriving at the White House, former President Herbert Hoover is greeted by President Truman, who is seeking Hoover's advice on the administration of food relief in Europe. President Hoover had vast experience in this field during World War I.

HOW CAN YOU KEEP THEM OFF OF THE FARM AFTER THEY'VE SEEN D.C.

Harry S. Truman got back his boyhood home when he and his brother chipped in $20,000. His mother defaulted on the interest payment and lost the 287-acre farm in 1940.

CABARET DES TROUPES ALLIEES BIGGEST SOCIAL EVENT IN PARIS SINCE LIBERATION

Thousands of G.I.'s rubbed elbows with a bejewelled host of celebrities and royalty as they gathered for the gala opening of the Cabaret des Troupes Alliées. Marlene Dietrich dazzled the audience with her singing and dancing while Maurice Chevalier won everyone's heart with his risqué banter and a medley of U.S. song hits.

THE CHECK'S IN THE MAIL

Party girl **Elsa Maxwell** was found guilty by Manhattan's City Court of owing $2,980.74 on a jewelry bill. The $996.47 balance in her checking account was immediately turned over as partial payment of the judgment.

FRANKLY, WE DO GIVE A DAMN
Vivian Leigh Wins Right-To-Work Court Battle Against David Selznik

STARS GATHER AT STATLER HOTEL FOR MARCH OF DIMES BALL AND TO CELEBRATE FDR'S BIRTHDAY

Joe E. Brown, who entertains servicemen in every theatre of war, delivers a few funny remarks.

Beautiful Jane Wyman is one of the invited stars.

Mrs. Roosevelt, surrounded by family and friends, makes the first cut in the President's birthday cake.

WHAT A YEAR IT WAS!

1945

FAMOUS BIRTHS

Maud Adams
David Brenner
Eric Clapton
Rita Coolidge
David Dukes
Donna Fargo
Mia Farrow
Jose Feliciano
Teri Garr
Goldie Hawn
John Heard
Linda Hunt
John Lithgow
Steve Martin
Bette Midler
Melba Moore
Anne Murray
Jessye Norman
Itzhak Perlman
Rob Reiner
Diane Sawyer
Tom Selleck
Carly Simon
Rod Stewart
Stephen Stills
Frederica von Stade
Henry Winkler
Neil Young

AMERICA'S HANDSOME MEN

Gary Cooper
Philip Merivale
Admiral Richard E. Byrd
Gregor Piatigorsky
Frederic March
Lt. Gen. Mark Clark
Raymond Massey
Gen. Douglas MacArthur
Cary Grant
Paul V. McNutt

DECEMBER 21

General **George S. Patton**, America's most cantankerous war hero, dies in a Heidelberg army hospital as a result of complications from injuries sustained in a car accident. Master of tank warfare, Patton was relieved of his command and removed from his position of prominence by General Eisenhower due to inappropriate comments made to reporters. Patton had earlier slapped a soldier in a military hospital for what he believed was cowardice when, in fact, the young soldier was suffering from battle fatigue.

• PASSINGS •

JANUARY: Major **Glenn Miller** is reported missing while on a flight from England to Paris.

APRIL 18: War correspondent **Ernie Pyle**, whose coverage of the war endeared him to the G.I.'s he wrote about, is killed by Japanese machine gun fire.

Founder of Hadassah, the women's Zionist organization, **Henrietta Szold**, dies at 84.

Amy Marcy Cheney Beach, the first woman composer to have a work performed by the New York Symphony (1892), dies at 77.

HUMAN INTEREST

Pan Am Announces
Round-The-World Flight
In 88 Hours At A
Fare Of $700

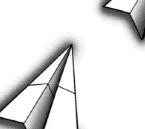

The B-29 Superfortress Breaks All
Records, Crossing The U.S. In Five
Hours, 27 Minutes

New Postwar Airplane Dream Kitchen
Will Allow Service Of Hot And Cold Foods
Prepared On The Plane

1945

january Truman Recommends Draft Of Registered Nurses

february Federal Grand Jury To Investigate Cigarette Black Market

march House Of Representatives Passes First Bill To Draft Women

april French Women Vote For First Time

august U.S. Office of Censorship Ceases Operations

O.K. first find your I.Q.
then figure out the wartime stamp guide below

I.Q. RATING	TYPE NAME
0-25	Idiot
25-50	Imbecile
50-70	Moron
70-80	Borderline
80-90	Dull or Retarded
90-110	Normal
110-120	Superior
120-130	Very Superior
130 & Over	Gifted

All RED and BLUE stamps in War Ration Book 4 are WORTH 10 POINTS EACH. RED and BLUE TOKENS are used to make CHANGE for RED and BLUE stamps only when purchase is made.
IMPORTANT! POINT VALUES of BROWN and GREEN STAMPS are NOT changed.

PILOT SURVIVES 2000 FOOT FREE FALL INTO OCEAN

Miraculously, Marine Corps pilot, James Gilbert Percy, suffers only a few broken bones after his parachute fails to open at 2,000 feet. He is picked up out of the ocean 24 hours later and expects to fly again.

BACK FROM THE WILD BLUE YONDER

Sixty-five battle bombers arrive at Bradley Field from Europe with more than a thousand veterans of the continental air war.

Overjoyed to be home again, this pilot kisses the ground.

After 30-day furloughs, the men are trained in new heavy bombers and then sent to Japan along with their mascots.

HERE COMES THE BRIDE

Ten thousand American servicemen stationed down under marry Australian women who become friends while awaiting transportation to the United States.

Some of those waiting to sail make visits to the American war cemetery in Sydney to pay tribute to our soldiers.

G.I. ON THE HOOK FOR FOUR WIVES

To overcome his loneliness, an American G.I. stationed on a remote island in the Pacific traded fishhooks for four wives. His dilemma: to get the Veteran's Administration to allow him to bring them to America and collect extra money under the G.I. Bill of Rights.

Some Day My Prince Will Come... *Maybe*

While American women worry about the shortage of eligible men and becoming spinsters, population experts and sociologists are worried too and warn of the following likely ramifications:

1 Dramatic drop in birth rate.

2 Deterioration of moral standards.

3 Increase in prostitution, illegitimacy and emotional disorders among women of marriageable age.

4 Economic dislocation as women compete for men's jobs.

5 Growth of polygamy to compensate for the diminished male base.

COUPLING & *un*COUPLING

Number of Marriages:	Number of Divorces:
1,613,000	**485,000**

Divorce Suits Filed Reach New High – Record Number Of Decrees Granted In Reno

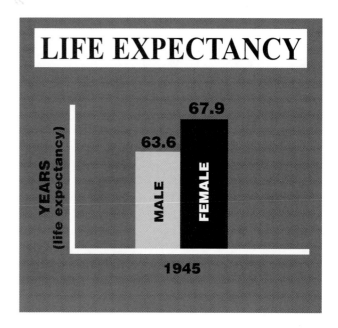

LIFE EXPECTANCY

63.6 MALE — 67.9 FEMALE

YEARS (life expectancy)

1945

1945

1945 ADVERTISEMENT

Tested in hospital nurseries!
Wonderfully effective!

Try new

Johnson's Baby Lotion –
ANTISEPTIC

**Truman Recommends
First Comprehensive
Health Insurance Plan**

**Housing Critically
Inadequate To Meet Needs
Of Postwar America**

Mother—welcome Johnson's Baby Lotion! The new, better way to take care of baby's skin —tested in hospitals!

There's a scientific reason why Johnson's Baby Lotion *agrees* with sensitive baby skin—helps prevent irritations like diaper rash and heat rash.

This smooth, snow-white lotion is an *emulsion* of specially compounded mineral oil, soothing lanolin, and water. Leaves a light film that's a *network*—not a solid layer. Perspiration can get out— but urine can't get in to irritate. And the antiseptic—being in a lotion base—can *work better!*

And just imagine—how much nicer Johnson's Baby Lotion is to use. Never sticky or messy. Hospital nurses say it's a *pleasure* to smooth on baby—after his bath or at diaper changes.

Doesn't this sound like a new day dawning for you and your baby? For *both* your sakes, get a bottle of Johnson's Baby Lotion today!

**Crime Increases
After Wartime
Decline**

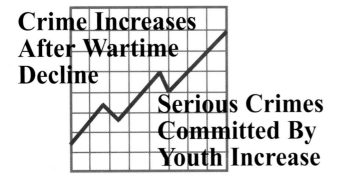

**Serious Crimes
Committed By
Youth Increase**

Made by the makers of
Johnson's Baby Powder

Johnson's
Baby Lotion
ANTISEPTIC
50¢ *Johnson & Johnson*

JAPANESE ALIENS ARE SENT HOME FROM AMERICA

Japanese men and women who renounced their United States citizenship during the war, along with diplomats arrested in Europe, are deported to their homeland from Seattle, Washington.

Included are the former Japanese ambassador to Berlin and Japanese aliens who lived in America for over 30 years. Many have expressed hope they can help in the reconstruction of their shattered homeland.

To a Baby Born in the Year of Victory

It's a great world you're born into, and just how lucky you are you'll never know till *you grow up!*

You will enjoy life in a world at peace. Your dad and mother's generation paid a high price to win this better world for you. This is one of the things, big and little things, they do for your welfare—for parents are that way.

That's why they are buying you a Victory Bond. For they want you to have every advantage to enjoy this better world when you face life on your own. Like the other things they do for you, some day you will wonder at their thoughtfulness and thank them with gratitude in your heart.

* * *

Ten years from now every $75 you invest in Victory Bonds will become $100 for that baby of yours. No investment can be safer— your Government stands behind every bond. Victory Bond drive will start October 29th.

Give your baby the right start in life—
Buy **VICTORY BONDS NOW!**

© 1945. G. P. C.

A message to the mothers and fathers of America on behalf of the Victory Loan from

Gerber's Baby Foods

FREMONT, MICH.—OAKLAND, CAL.

CEREALS • STRAINED FOODS • CHOPPED FOODS

TALLEST BUILDING IN THE U.S.

Empire State Building – New York City
102 Stories, 1,250 Feet

Lightning Hits New York City's Empire State Building During Electrical Storm

NEITHER RAIN, NOR SNOW, NOR *CENSORSHIP...*

The District Court of Appeals in Washington, D.C. handed down two important decisions barring post office interference with delivery of two pamphlets: *"Report on Contraceptive Material"* and *"Preparing for Marriage."*

The Statue of Liberty is having her floodlighting system overhauled in preparation for Allied victory celebrations.

A Hard Pill To Swallow
• • • • • • • • • • • • • • • •
Connecticut & Massachusetts Prevent Physicians From Prescribing Birth Control

ƒebruary 1
• • • • • • • • • • • • • • • • •
New Lincoln Tunnel Connecting New York And New Jersey Opens Today

OUIJA BOARD

CONSIDERED WARTIME FAD

The popularity of occult devices, including the Ouija Board, is a result of wartime anxiety, according to a psychology professor at Columbia University, and not a new phenomenon. World War I saw a sharp rise in seances and other "magic" methods of predicting the future and communicating with the dead. The professor predicts an end to the craze within a year.

Your Left, Your Left – Or Is It Your Right, Your Right

In preparation for the takeover of ground defense of an American base in the South Pacific, an Australian unit learns to drive on the right side of the road, while at the same time, as a courtesy, the Americans learn to drive on the left. The traffic jam is monumental.

PUT THIS IN YOUR SPELLING BEE BONNET

In Wales, when the wartime ban on railway-station signs was removed, a stationmaster restored his town's 30-foot long sign:

Llanfairpwllgwyngogerychrynbwllllandysiliogogogoch

Midnight Curfew Instituted Throughout U.S.

"Black Market" Dealings Sweep Europe

Washington Ends 35 m.p.h. Speed Limit

Family Allowance Introduced In Britain

U.S. Supreme Court Strikes Down Detention Of Loyal U.S. Citizens In U.S./Japanese Test Cases

WHEN THE LIGHTS COME ON AGAIN

Lights are once again turned on in Paris on the Arc de Triomphe and Cathedral of Notre Dame for the first time since the war began.

Shoe Rationing Ends In The U.S.

Meat & Butter Rationing Ends In The U.S.

Tire Rationing Ends In The U.S.

CAMP FIRE GIRLS

Camp Fire Girls International Friendship Program Observes "Share The Food Day" To Help Feed The Needy

President Truman Named Honorary President Of The Camp Fire Girls

The U.S. presidential flag is redesigned. The white star in each corner has been eliminated, and the eagle faces right, toward the olive branch of peace, held in the right talon.

HEALING HANDS ACROSS THE SEA

Boy Scouts of America Theme:

"Scouts of the World – Brothers Together."

THERE'S A LOT OF STEAK IN THAT THERE COW

Cattlemen attending the National Western Livestock Show witness the highest price ever paid for a U.S. beef animal – $50,000 for a prize Hereford.

SATISFYING THE SWEET TOOTH

5¢ candy bar sales surpass all other forms of candy for second year in a row.

According to the U.S. Department of Agriculture, rubbing a piece of candle wax or paraffin on the heels and toes of stockings before wearing makes them last four times longer before holes appear.

DID YOU HEAR THE ONE ABOUT...

A major insurance company settled two unusual claims – one for a broken wrist sustained by a woman while wiggling into her girdle, the other for an exploding glass eye.

Experiments Reveal Roses Cut Late In The Afternoon Keep Petals Longer

❄ **Coldest** ❄ **Winter In 25 Years Hits East Coast** ❄

The American Red Cross reaches a peak of activity during the war. They prepare 27,000,000 food packages for prisoners of war and process 110,000 communications.

Deepest Hole In The World: Texas Oil Well, 3 Miles Down

YANKEE JOKES ALWAYS LEAVE THEM LAUGHING

Britons and Canadians agree that American humor is funnier than that of any other nation.

New Words

Atomic Age

The new age dominated by atomic energy, ushered in with the dropping of the first atomic bomb, August 6, 1945.

Blow Job

A jet-propelled plane.

Butcherette

Female butcher.

Disintegrator

Secret weapon to oppose kamikaze attacks.

D.P.

Displaced person.

Electric Blanket

Blanket made by General Electric Company, electrically heated and automatically controlled.

Fleet Admiral

Admiral of the fleet.

Flight Test

To test an airplane in flight.

Flying Boxcar Bomb

U.S. name for the 700-lb., 5-foot-long spigot mortar of the Japanese.

Formation Stick

An electronically operated control stick which makes manipulation of a plane much easier and thus decreases fatigue to pilots.

Fraternize

To deal socially with members of an enemy nation, especially with women.

Genocide

Extermination of racial and national groups.

Homing Pigeon

Button to identify discharged servicemen.

Meateasy

Place where black market meat can be bought.

Hubba, Hubba

Exclamation of enthusiastic approval.

Mickey Mouse Money

Valueless Japanese money in the Philippines.

Pinpoint

To determine precisely.

Inspectoscope

An x-ray device used by the armed forces to discover illegal objects in packages sent home by servicemen.

Plutonium

Element #94, which results when radioactive neptunium breaks down with the emission of an electron which changes one of its neutrons into a proton; not found naturally.

Jungle Rot

Any of several tropical skin diseases.

Kamikaze

A suicide attack by a Japanese plane.

Pre-atomic

Before August 6, 1945, the date of the atomic bombing of Hiroshima.

Manhattan Project

The atomic bomb project.

May Day

Call for help.

Set-aside

Materials, such as meat, canned goods and vegetables, set-aside by order of the government for its use.

Under Wraps

Censored, secret.

Strato-suit

A suit, pressurized and heated by electricity, which makes it possible for flyers to be comfortable at altitudes as high as 80,000 feet; oxygen is supplied through a special headpiece.

Vista Dome

A glass-enclosed section, slightly raised above the top of a railway coach to enable its occupants to see in any direction.

Stratovision

Method of using planes in the stratosphere to broadcast television.

V-J Day

Victory over Japan – much of the world considers August 15, 1945 to be V-J Day. In the United States, however, President Truman declares September 2, 1945, the date of the formal surrender, V-J Day.

Talking Book

A recording of a reading of a book for use by the blind.

Terror Bombing

Deliberate bombing for terror effects with hope of shortening a war.

War-weary

A plane beyond repair; also, one whose great damage at the front requires it to be sent home for repairs.

Top Secret

A security classification used by the armed forces and the diplomatic corps to denote material of the utmost secrecy.

Werewolf

Member of a German underground organization opposing the Allies.

A special process keeps Kleenex

Luxuriously Soft – Dependably Strong

Only Kleenex has the Serv-a-Tissue Box that serves up just one double-tissue at a time!

YOUR NOSE KNOWS – THERE'S ONLY ONE KLEENEX

In these days of shortages we can't promise you all the Kleenex you want, at all times. But we do promise you this: we'll always keep Kleenex the finest quality tissue that can be made!

There is <u>only one</u> KLEENEX*

*T. M. Reg. U. S. Pat. Off.

1945

A•Choo
Anatomy Of The Common Cold

Peak : December
Lowest : July
Common Cause : Sudden drops in temperature accompanied by rain

COLD FACTS

- Office workers have more colds than factory workers, with women catching more colds than men.
- Fewer colds are found in air-conditioned plants.
- More colds start on Monday than any other day.
- More colds are caught in smoking rooms.
- Vitamin C has some value in cold prevention.

PROFILE OF A NEUROTIC, CARELESS SMOKER

- Messes up cigarette package
- Taps cigarette in a staccato manner to get rid of loose tobacco
- Uses ashtray excessively
- Flicks ashes on the carpet
- Leaves lighted cigarettes on table tops
- Burns holes in furniture
- Blows smoke in your face

1945

WAR DOGS GO HOME

After serving a tour of duty overseas, canine veterans are sent to a dog dude ranch for reorientation.

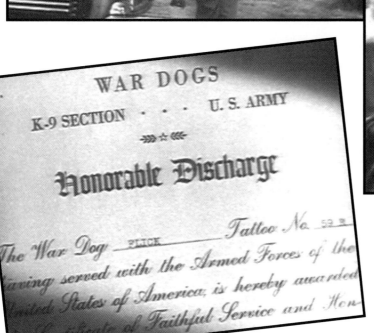

Debriefing completed, these loyal canines return to their families.

Only Living Quadruplet Calves Born In Dyer, Kentucky

Philadelphia Zoo Loses Last Maned Wolf In Captivity To Kidney Failure

WHAT A YEAR IT WAS!

BUSINESS

BUSINESS OVERVIEW

Throughout 1945, until victory is achieved, first priority is given to winning the war. Businessmen are kept informed through their Chambers of Commerce of changing wartime regulations and are asked to share their opinions and perspectives with government officials.

With Japan's surrender, America's vast industrial machine has the overwhelming challenge of shifting from manufacturing war materials to peacetime production.

Milton Snavely Hershey, chairman of the board of the Hershey Chocolate Company, dies at 88.

That <u>new</u> washer of yours

...the purchase of a lifetime!

Women want washers more than any other household appliance.

Six million women are waiting eagerly to buy.

Now after nearly four years, new washers are again being produced—although the supply at first may be limited.

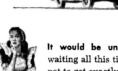

 **It would be unfortunate,** after waiting all this time, if you were not to get exactly *the* washer you want. For this is truly the purchase of a lifetime. This *should* be the last washer you will ever have to buy.

Do not be dazzled by "looks" alone. Look deeper—and think deeper. Many of the new washers will be beautifully styled in today's modern trend. Some will not look like washers at all. But remember, styles change—and this is the purchase of a lifetime. Not a mere ornament, but a working partner.

The new Maytag is handsome—because it looks like what it is!—the most nearly perfect laundering instrument we have ever built. Its beauty grows out of the job it has to do—like the beauty of a skyscraper or a suspension bridge.

It looks capable, because it *is* capable—of handling the biggest washing, with ease and speed. It looks rugged, because it *is* rugged—built to accomplish that washing job, week after week through the years, for a lifetime of faithful service. The true beauty of **the** Maytag is in its beauty of results.

The swift, sure, *Gyrafoam action:* exclusive with Maytag, gets the dirt and grime out of excessively soiled fabrics—yet handles your fine lingerie, laces, and nylons with the gentleness of delicate fingers.

The big, square Maytag *cast aluminum tub* takes biggest washings—keeps water hotter, longer! The Maytag *sediment zone* traps the dirt from water, so that dirt is not washed back into the clothes.

The famous Maytag Damp Drier with its firm-and-flexible rolls, is gentle and efficient, swings to any position, and is finger-tip controlled for utmost safety!

Maytag actually *does* build washers for the *service of a lifetime.* Hundreds of thousands of Maytags, serving valiantly today, have been in constant use for almost a lifetime already. Maytag has built more washers than any other manufacturer. That is why we believe your purchase of a Maytag is the safest investment your washer money will buy.

The Maytag Company, Newton, Iowa

A ***Maytag*** IS WORTH WAITING FOR

WOMEN'S CLOTHING

Bra	$ 2.50
Dress	16.95
Satin Robe	17.00
Shoes	8.95
Stockings	1.95
Taffeta Dress	8.95
Wool Jersey Dress	50.00

MEN'S CLOTHING

Dress Shirt	$ 2.50
Dress Shoes	8.50
Raincoat	12.00
Socks	.50
Suspenders	1.60
Tie	1.50
Wool Suit	40.00

Bacon (lb.)	$ .41
Bread (lb.)	.09
Butter (lb.)	.51
Chuck Roast (lb.)	.28
Coffee (lb.)	.30
Eggs (doz.)	.58
Flour (5 lb.)	.32
Margarine (lb.)	.24
Milk (1/2 gal., delivered)	.31
Oranges (doz.)	.48
Pork Chops (lb.)	.37
Potatoes (10 lb.)	.48
Round Steak (lb.)	.41
Sugar (5 lb.)	.33
Tomatoes (#303 can)	.10

Record Player

$189.00

WHAT A YEAR IT WAS!

Camera Film (8 exp.)
25¢

Deodorant
(jar)
39¢

ELECTRIC ALARM CLOCK
$4.95

Electric Iron
$4.45

After Shave Lotion
$1.00

Aspirin
25¢

Bath Towel
59¢

Cough Drops
(box)
5¢

Calculator
(with automatic division)
$95.00

Soap
15¢

PAINT
interior, 1 gal.
$2.98

YOUR RATIONING GUIDE

ITEMS	POINTS
American Cheddar Cheese (lb.)	8
Baby Foods (4-1/2 oz. jar)	1
Butter (lb.)	16
Canned Milk (lb.)	1
Ham (lb.)	7
Peaches (16 oz. can)	18
Pineapple Juice (46 oz. can)	22
Porterhouse Steak (lb.)	12
Tomato Catsup (14 oz.)	15

MOTOR OIL
35¢

Soda Pop
5¢

Tampons
(box)
20¢

Toothbrush
23¢

Toothpaste **37¢**

ARCHITECTURE

THE OFFICE OF TOMORROW

- ■ The executive's glass-walled office will be on a revolving platform to take full advantage of sunlight.

- ■ Live conferences will be held through the use of television/telephone devices.

- ■ Mathematic calculations will be done on electronic devices.

- ■ Files will be retrieved electronically.

- ■ Germ-free air will result from special lighting.

HOME & HEARTH

Steel To Be Important Material In Prefabricated And "Package" House Of Tomorrow

•

Henry Kaiser Builds Mill In An Orange Grove— Hopes To Create New Way Of Life For Working People

•

"Postwar" House Changes Back To "Dream House" And "House Of Tomorrow"

•

New Type Of Refrigerator Stores Meats And Other Foods At Sub-Zero Temperatures

•

Imitation French Provincial, Tudor English, Ming Chinese And American Colonial Furniture Designs Fill American Homes

•

Ansly Radio Corporation Designs New Radio For Built-In Installation

•

New Thermostat Timer Designed To Regulate Heating Equipment

•

Edison General Electric Announces Automatic Washing Machines And Electric Tumble Dryers To Be Postwar Additions To Their Home Laundry Line

THE LOOK

❏ **Glass walls in living rooms merge the outdoors with the indoors.**

❏ **Eat-in kitchens make meal preparation more efficient and serving easier.**

❏ **Rooms serve several functions.**

❏ **Laundries and kitchens are combined.**

❏ **Walls are painted in lighter colors.**

❏ **Wall papers are of stripes, plaids and floral designs.**

MATERIALS

The scarcity of materials used in interior decoration is expected to abate in 1946-47. Previews of new designs are made available to the public through "advertising for the future."

❏ **Laminated construction is developed.**

❏ **Prefabricated steel panels are developed.**

❏ **Plastics become available for building use.**

❏ **Radiant heating becomes more fully recognized.**

❏ **Lumber replaces hundreds of thousands of tons of steel in large construction projects.**

❏ **Manufacturing of rugs and carpets is at a standstill.**

❏ **Prefabricated houses are sold by department stores.**

❏ **Antique furniture is in demand due to limited furniture production.**

*U*nder Sponsorship Of The Baking Industry, 18 States Have Now Adopted A Uniform Bill For Enrichment Of Family Flour And Bakers' Bread and Rolls

Back to Basics

OPA REGULATIONS LIFTED ON:

- Bird Cages • Horseshoes
- Artificial Grass
- Cat & Dog Beds • Ship Bells
- Poker Chip Racks

U.S. Supreme Court Rules Aluminum Co. Of America A Monopoly In 8-Year Trust Busting Suit

HERE'S TO HEALTH *And Economy*

Limited Production Of Alcoholic Beverages Permitted

Revenues From Alcoholic Beverages Greatest In History

AIR EXPRESS MAIL DELIVERY PLANS POSTWAR SERVICE EXPANSION

Interest Develops In Commercial Production Of Frozen Bakery Products

Gimbel's Sales Reach All Time High – Bernard Gimbel Predicts Best 100 Years Lie Ahead

Restrictions Lifted On Shoe Industry For Design And Creative Development

Nebraska

Becomes First State In The Union To Have All Its Power Companies Publicly Owned

New York State Passes Fair Employment Practices Act

Postwar Demands For Cotton Products Unmet

100,000 New York Workers Laid Off From War Jobs As Contracts End

Textile Workers Minimum Wage: $.55 Per Hour

EMPLOYMENT

WHAT A YEAR IT WAS!

3 Cheers for Mother

...AT THIS BUSY CHRISTMASTIME!

So much to do...so little time to do it! Why not let Campbell's Soups help you serve meals that are both time-saving and soundly nourishing? Have you some on hand — to see you through the Holidays?

Lunch is Served in Jig-time!

America's favorite soup...made according to Campbell's exclusive recipe from luscious sun-ripened tomatoes, blended with table butter and a touch of seasoning. Campbell's Tomato Soup is an ever-popular choice for a family lunch.

Supper's Ready in a Jiffy!

Here is a soup of tender garden peas blended with fine table butter into a velvet-smooth purée. Add milk instead of water to Campbell's Green Pea Soup, and you've an extra-rich and extra-nourishing cream of pea. This is a grand soup to build a simple but satisfying supper around.

Quick to Fix for Dinner!

And what an appetizing soup it is! Campbell's Consommé is made from beef slowly simmered till all the invigorating goodness is captured in a clear broth. This is just the soup to get dinner off to a good start — including the Christmas feast!

115

1945

SCIENCE & MEDICINE

NOBEL PRIZE WINNERS

PHYSICS
Wolfgang Pauli (U.S.)

CHEMISTRY
Artturi I. Virtanen (Finland)

MEDICINE
Ernst B. Chain, Sir Alexander Fleming, Sir Howard W. Florey (Great Britain)

AH, THEREIN LIES THE RUB

With trench foot, a mild frostbite with serious consequences if left untreated, affecting both Allied and enemy soldiers due to the cold, wet winter, the Russians come up with the best solution. Russian soldiers are paired off and required to massage each other's feet regularly. If one of the massage buddies gets trench foot, the other is severely disciplined.

8,000,000 Members Of The United States Army Are Inoculated Against Virus A and B Influenza

EXPERIMENTS ON ANIMALS REVEAL HOT BATHS MAY REDUCE MALE FERTILITY

WHAT A YEAR IT WAS!

An estimated 20,000,000 people worldwide are left handicapped at war's end. Excellent results are achieved in the treatment of paraplegics through advances in physical and occupational therapy.

THE WONDER DRUG

Penicillin Controls Removed Making It More Available

Penicillin Injections Make It Possible For Private Physicians To Treat Gonorrhea In Their Offices

Oral Administration Of Penicillin Gains Popularity

Benadryl Used In Treatment Of Various Allergy Conditions

Vitamin A Synthesized

Streptomycin Used Successfully In Treating Tuberculosis

Gamma Globulin Is Medical Science's Latest Weapon Against Measles And Infectious Hepatitis

1945

Drunk As A Skunk... er...CAT

Experiments performed on neurotic cats reveal that those made tipsy by alcohol lost their neurotic behavior but as they sobered up, the behavior reappeared.

"Neurotic"

HEADACHE THY NAME BE BEAUTY

Beautiful, intelligent, charming, sensitive women are particularly prone to migraine headaches, according to a professor on staff of the Mayo Clinic. The female migraine sufferer is usually petite, above average in intelligence and social skills, is decisive, idealistic, perfectionistic, and has unusual sensitivity to noises, bright lights and unpleasant odors. The combination of beauty, brains and sensitivity seems to be the combination of factors in nearly all women suffering from migraines.

Death Rate Of Working Women From Diseases Falls During War Years

Streptomycin Effectively Used To Treat Certain Bacteria Not Responsive To Penicillin

She's Engaged!

Infantry Officer from Kansas will wed Arkansas Girl Engagement of **BETTY JANE CANNON** to **H. W. SMITH, Jr.** has been announced by her parents

HER RING— a large and two small diamonds

"*POND'S IS MY CREAM*," Betty Jane Cannon says. She has one of the prettiest complexions you've ever seen.

● Betty Jane Cannon has unforgettable beauty that wings its way straight to your heart—as it did to the heart of her officer fiancé, now overseas.

Her complexion is porcelain-like in its smoothness, with a dewy, soft-smooth look —the look *so many* Pond's engaged girls seem to have!

"It's not just luck my skin is nice," Betty Jane says. "I don't give much time to it— but I do give it regular creamings with Pond's Cold Cream. I *love* Pond's—and I think it does lots for me."

This is how she uses Pond's:

She smooths plenty of fragrant Pond's Cold Cream over her face—throat, too—patting briskly to help soften and release dirt and make-up. Tissues off.

She rinses with *more* Pond's—swirling her cream-tipped fingers all around her face. Tissues again. "I enjoy this second creaming. It feels so good and it does such an *extra-special* cleansing, softening job," she says.

Use your Pond's Cold Cream this two-time way—every night, every morning, and for in-between clean-ups! It's no accident so many more women and girls use Pond's than any other face cream at any price. Ask for a *big* luxury jar. It has a grand wide top that lets you dip in with both hands at once!

She's Lovely! She uses Pond's!

SIGNING UP NURSES—Betty Jane helped at a Nurse Recruiting Information Center during the recent drive for nurses, answering questions, telling girls and women how and where they could give the greatest service. There are many nursing needs these days . . . Registered Graduate Nurses, Student Nurses, Trained Nurse's Aides, Home Nursing. Ask at your local hospital what *you* can best do.

A few of the many Pond's Society Beauties: Mrs. Alister McCormick · Princess Xenia · Mrs. Victor L. Drexel · The Lady Morris

Alcoholic Tendencies Are Not Inherited, According To Yale Study

Infantile Paralysis Outbreaks Reported Worldwide
··················
Infant Mortality Reaches New Low In U.S.

NEW TEST FOR PREGNANCY

By use of an electrocardiograph machine, which detects and records faint electrical impulses, Yale physicians have been able to determine pregnancy as early as the fourth month.

DDT Found Highly Toxic To Fish And Frogs

DIG YOUR TEETH INTO THIS

American Dental Association establishes plan providing dental services to low income groups.

Castration Method Of Breast Cancer Treatment Produces Discouraging Results

WHAT A YEAR IT WAS!

When Grandmothers get together...

They may not see eye to eye as to which side of the family can claim Winkie's pug nose or his angelic disposition . . . but there'll be no doubt about their complete agreement on the goodness of Irradiated Carnation Milk for his feeding formula.

Carnation is just perfect for babies! It's *homogenized* and *sterilized* for easier digestion and safety, and it's *irradiated* for extra "sunshine" vitamin D . . . things that *older* children need too!

They'll *get* them—and *like* them—when they *eat* Carnation in delicious milk-rich dishes. Carnation's fine recipes are easy to make . : . and *so* good to eat!

No wonder these grandmothers know what they're talking about : : : they raised *their* children on Carnation Milk, too.

What a fine old record for Carnation!

CHOCOLATE PEPPERMINT CAKE
A Valentine favorite!

¼ cup shortening
1 cup sugar
1 egg, slightly beaten
1 teaspoon vanilla
1¼ cups cake flour
1½ teaspoons baking powder
¼ teaspoon soda
¼ teaspoon salt
¼ cup cocoa
½ cup Carnation Milk, diluted with ½ cup water
2 drops oil of peppermint

Cream shortening and sugar. Add egg and vanilla. Sift flour and measure. Resift with the other dry ingredients. Add flour mixture and milk alternately to the first mixture. Beat well. Add oil of peppermint. Bake in greased 8-inch square pan in a moderate oven of 350° F. about 45 minutes. Frost with Cream Cheese Icing. Serves 8 to 10. Double recipe for 2-layer cake. Decorate with red frosting and peppermint stick candy.

FREE! "GROWING UP WITH MILK." A 48-page booklet chuck full of delicious milk-rich dishes for all the family, with special help for each age group. You'll want to try every easy-to-make recipe . . . your family will want a "repeat" on every one, time and again! Address Dept. L-44, Carnation Company, Milwaukee 2, Wis., Toronto, Ont.

CREAM CHEESE ICING

1 3-ounce package cream cheese
1 tablespoon Carnation Milk, undiluted
2 cups confectioners' sugar
1 teaspoon vanilla

Blend cheese and milk. Stir in sugar and vanilla, and beat until smooth. Double recipe for 2-layer cake.

IRRADIATED Carnation Milk

"FROM CONTENTED COWS"

TUNE' IN THE CARNATION "CONTENTED HOUR"   MONDAY EVENINGS, NBC NETWORK

121

Eye Banks Are Established

LOOK INTO MY EYES DAHLING

According to a statement issued by the New York State Optometric Association, ring formations in the lens of the eye are an indication of how old you are. *Watch those close-ups, ladies!*

HOT TIP

The temperature of the lighted end of a cigarette is slightly above the melting point of aluminum or magnesium (1200 to 1325 degrees Fahrenheit).

ALARMING INCREASE IN HEART DISEASE AMONG YOUNGER PEOPLE

SURGICAL PROCEDURES IMPROVE

Nitrous Oxide Gas Declared Unsafe

The U.S. Has Only 3,000 Psychiatrists

Infectious Hepatitis Becomes Widespread

1945 ADVERTISEMENT

What's wrong with this picture of Nurse Bradley?

NURSE BRADLEY just shouldn't be in this picture at all. Because her patient shouldn't be sick enough to require a special nurse.

A while ago he began feeling upset. He made up his own mind it was "just a touch of indigestion." The condition persisted. He kept on dosing himself with what he believed was "just the stuff for it." He neglected to see his doctor. So his trouble had a chance to develop into something really serious. Serious enough for a hospital bed. And Nurse Bradley's services. And lots of his doctor's time.

A shame. Because there's a serious shortage of medical manpower these days. A large number of our doctors and nurses are in military service.

So . . . help your doctor save his time. The very best way to save your doctor's time is to make use of his services the minute trouble arises. Never indulge in self-diagnosis. See your doctor early, in time for him to head off more serious trouble. And help him further by doing these three things:

GO TO HIM—whenever you are able. House visits take time when someone else may need him urgently.

KEEP YOUR APPOINTMENT promptly; make it at his convenience so that he can plan his crowded hours better.

FOLLOW HIS ADVICE TO THE LETTER—so that your trouble doesn't drag on, get complicated, or need extra attention.

ONE OF A SERIES of messages published as a public service by Wyeth Incorporated, Philadelphia...relied upon by your physician and druggist for pharmaceuticals, nutritional products, and biologicals—including penicillin and blood plasma.

Wyeth

HELP YOUR DOCTOR SAVE HIS TIME!

123

INVENTIONS

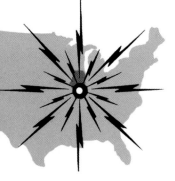

Color separations

for making printing plates are transmitted from Europe via radio to the Chicago Tribune, allowing them to publish a full-color, full-page illustration of the Big Three – Roosevelt, Stalin and Churchill.

EASTMAN KODAK DEVELOPS AERIAL PHOTOGRAPHY LENS FOR MILITARY USE

Fairchild Camera Introduces Camera For Photographing Radar Images

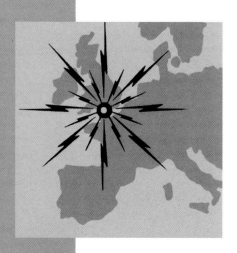

PEACETIME USE FOR THE WALKIE-TALKIE

The Federal Communications Commission announces plans for a new proposed frequency allocation for "Citizens Radio." Non-technical people will be licensed to operate radio telephones for communicating with civilian-owned and operated stations.

PEACETIME USE OF RADAR TO MAKE AIRPORTS SAFER

The use of radar to make postwar air travel safer is the subject of research by the Civil Aeronautics Administration. One proposal is the creation of radar control towers which would permit tracking of aircraft on screens. Hazardous conditions, from pilot error to fog-bound air-fields to exact position of other aircraft, would be detected immediately.

PEACETIME USES FOR MICROWAVES EXPLORED

Radio engineers are impressing U.S. citizens with the potential postwar applications of microwaves.

DISCOVERIES

ROADS WITH REFLECTIVE PAVEMENT ARE THOUGHT TO BE NEEDED FOR DRIVER SAFETY

DDT-Laced House Paint Continues To Be Lethal To Flies Two Months After Application

Photofluorography Is Introduced For Use In Fighting Tuberculosis

smaller
IS BETTER
According to a report released by the U.S. Department of Agriculture, small oranges produce sweeter juice with a higher vitamin C content than the larger ones.

Flexible Plastic Bags Invented For Packaging Foods

World's Largest Plane, Douglas C-74 Globemaster, Is Tested

A sickle, traced to Ur, the birthplace of Abraham, father of the Jews, is discovered by an excavation team dating the community to 5,000 to 6,000 B.C.– 2,000 years earlier than previous calculations.

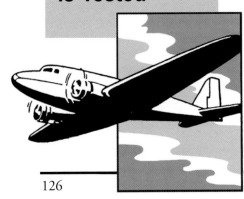

WHAT A YEAR IT WAS!

Coming Soon...

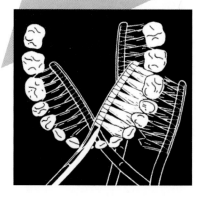

Grand Rapids, Michigan Is First U.S. City To Introduce Fluoride Into Its Drinking Water As Tooth Decay Prevention

• • • • • • • • • •

In the future, tooth decay will be prevented by brushing with toothpaste containing anti-cavity amino acids.

HOW'S THIS FOR YOUR SWEET TOOTH

Glycyrrhizin, found in licorice, is declared 50 times sweeter than cane sugar. Safe levels of usage to be determined.

Adrenaline Is Used In Cure And Possible Prevention Of Malaria

Benzedrine
Introduced
As Appetite
Suppressant

⇒ PASSINGS ⇐

SIMON LAKE,
father of the submarine, dies at 78.

Sir JOHN AMBROSE FLEMING,
one of the people responsible for the introduction of the telephone and wireless in England, dies at 95.

ROBERT H. GODDARD,
the engineer who developed the basic inventions that made rockets usable as weapons and for space exploration, dies at 62.

YOU'LL TAKE YOUR
EASE IN STYLE . . .

There's a *Ford* in your future!

Some day—when America's biggest job is done—peace will return. And with it will come a new Ford car that's big, roomy and sturdy.

. . . Then you'll have the kind of gentle ride you've always hoped for. So smooth. So packed with comfort. In front seat or back, you'll find yourself at ease, relaxed.

. . . But that's not all! Many other refinements will be found in this new Ford. Smart, improved styling that will have a youthful air. A new richness, both inside and out. And, of course, the famous thrift and reliability that have always been traditional with Ford cars.

. . . When the time comes, we'll be ready to start production plans. Meanwhile, however, the full Ford resources are being used to help bring Victory closer.

FORD MOTOR COMPANY

"STARS OF THE FUTURE". Listen to the new Ford musical program on all Blue Network stations. Every Friday night—8:00 E.W.T., 7:00 C.W.T., 9:00 M.W.T., 8:30 P.W.T.

THE COW STOPS HERE

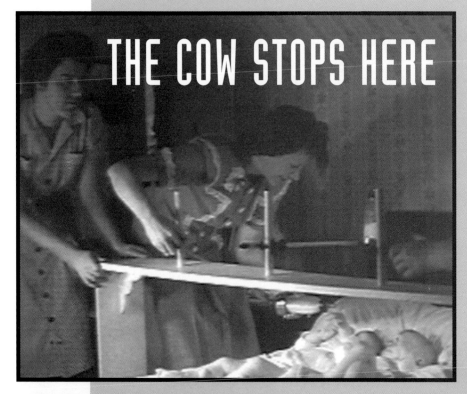

Modern production methods invade the home of Mr. & Mrs. Raymond McCloud of Weymouth, Mass. Necessity being the mother of invention, Papa McCloud dreamed up a universal feeder for his hungry triplets, ensuring that they don't have to stand in line for their milk.

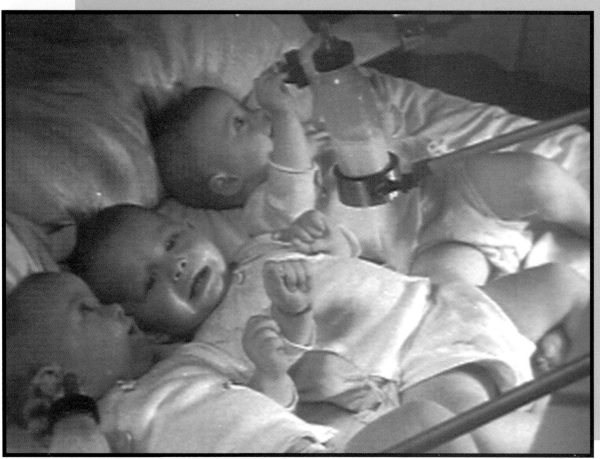

"Ginny Simms, just look what you've done to Elmer!" giggled Elsie

"WHY, ELSIE!" gasped Ginny Simms, "what have I done to Elmer?"

"Just what haven't you done?" laughed Elsie, the Borden Cow. "Elmer's been rumbling up and down the scales ever since he heard you were the star of Borden's new radio show! His ambition is to be the next swoon king!"

"And what's so thundering funny about that?" bellowed Elmer, the bull, leaning out of Signor Scalpone's window. "When I cut loose with my baritone, the ladies swoon by the herd! I *send* them! I knock 'em *cold!*"

"Then you certainly can't be on Ginny's program,"

teased Elsie. "We don't want folks to be out cold when we tell them about *Borden's Homogenized Milk.* It has cream and Vitamin D in every sip."

"Borden's! Borden's! Borden's!" groaned Elmer. "Why don't you get a new line? Why not put a fellow with a *fresh* viewpoint on your program—*me,* for instance?"

"Now, Elmer," soothed Elsie, "it's no good hinting. Ginny has really big stars on her show—some even bigger and funnier than you, dear."

"But, Elsie," protested Ginny, "I think Elmer's *delightful!* It's just that you've got to *see* him to appreciate him. Now, if this were television, Elmer could show folks how men really go for Borden's Liederkranz Cheese! It's a grand, robust cheese treat—with soft creamy center and good-to-eat golden crust!"

"Meanwhile, the *announcer,*" suggested Elsie, "reminds everybody that all *Borden's Fine Cheeses* are wonderful 'buys' for your points and pennies."

"*Break it up, women!*" roared Elmer, "and let's get back to radio. Trouble with you folks is you don't know a good bet when you see one."

"Why, darling," chirped Elsie, "the very best bet in

these days of food shortages is the new, richer chocolate flavored *Hemo.* This glorious food drink is *teeming* with vitamins and minerals everybody needs."

"*Vitamins and minerals!*" exploded Elmer. "What have they got to do with radio? Ever hear any of the GI's Ginny sings to twice a week yell for vitamins and minerals?"

"No, Elmer," laughed Ginny. "But I *have* heard them yell for ice cream. It's the favorite refreshment in Army *and* Navy."

"And *Borden's Ice Cream* is the real, old-fashioned

kind the boys—and everybody—*love,*" added Elsie. "It's a delicious, nourishing treat at any time. Real pep-boosting, too."

"Then you two better lay off it," slyly needled Elmer. "You're already too peppy about changing the subject. If I can't sing, and I can't tell jokes on the Borden show, why can't I be one of the war veterans Ginny interviews? Tell me that!"

"I'll tell you," chuckled Elsie, "because you haven't had a weapon in your hoof since the battle of Bull

Run. Seriously, dear, you were a grownup when Ginny's veterans were getting *Borden's Evaporated Milk* in their infant formulas."

"Speaking of Borden's Evaporated," suggested Ginny, "shouldn't we have the announcer on the radio show tell everybody that this fine milk has more Vitamin D than ever—400 units per reconstituted quart!"

"*Say!*" blurted Elmer, "I could do that just dandy. I could—"

"Elmer! Elmer!" chided Ginny, "you can't just become an announcer over night. Announcers must go through weeks of training. They—"

"*Weeks of training!*" roared Elmer. "I've had *years!* Ever since the fatal day Elsie mooed 'yes,' I've been trained to say, '*If it's Borden's, it's GOT to be good!*'"

— if it's Borden's, it's got to be good!

TUNE IN

GINNY SIMMS

IN A

GREAT **NEW** RADIO SHOW

with comedy guest stars!

★

New time, new station Friday evenings—CBS

E.W.T. 7:30   M.W.T. 7:00
C.W.T. 6:30   P.W.T. 6:00

© The Borden Company

ENTERTAINMENT

JACK BENNY opens fan mail, including one from Fred Allen who writes: *"I can't stand Jack Benny because he can't stand me more than I can't stand him."*

1945

AMERICA CELEBRATES A PEACETIME HOLIDAY SEASON

In New York, 2 million people turn out to watch the first holiday parade since the war began.

The lights come on again on Santa Claus Lane in Hollywood as stars turn out to kick off holiday festivities.

Jack Benny and his sidekick, Rochester, greet the smiling crowd.

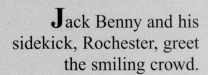

Edgar Bergen and Charlie McCarthy join the parade of stars.

FILMS OF 1945

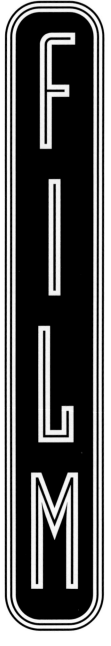

FILM

A Royal Scandal

A Song To Remember

A Tree Grows In Brooklyn

Anchors Aweigh

Beachhead To Berlin

BELLE OF THE YUKON

Brief Encounter

Can't Help Singing

Colonel Blimp

Flame Of Barbary Coast

God Is My Co-Pilot

Hangover Square

HERE COME THE WAVES

Hollywood Canteen

House On 92nd Street

Ivan The Terrible

Kiss And Tell

LAURA

Love Letters

Meet Me In St. Louis

Mildred Pierce

Ministry Of Fear

Mr. Emmanuel

MURDER, MY SWEET

National Velvet

Objective Burma

Rhapsody In Blue

See My Lawyer

S P E L L B O U N D

STATE FAIR

Sunday Dinner For A Soldier

Tall In The Saddle

The Corn Is Green

The Enchanted Cottage

The Fighting Lady

The Keys Of The Kingdom

The Lost Weekend

The Picture Of Dorian Gray

THE SUSPECT

The Thin Man Goes Home

THE THREE CABALLEROS

The Woman In The Window

Thirty Seconds Over Tokyo

This Man's Navy

Those Endearing Young Charms

To Have And Have Not

WINGED VICTORY

Without Love

Wuthering Heights

YANKS ON LUZON

WHAT A YEAR IT WAS!

1945

MOVIE STAR SOLDIERS RETURN TO HOLLYWOOD AFTER TOUR OF DUTY

Jean Pierre Aumont
Gene Autry
Lew Ayres
Bruce Cabot
John Carroll
Jackie Coogan
Henry Fonda

Clark Gable
Louis Hayward
Van Heflin
William Holden
William Lundigan
Victor Mature
Robert Montgomery

John Payne
Tyrone Power
Gene Raymond
Ronald Reagan
Cesar Romero
Buddy Rogers
James Stewart

NEW SCREEN PERSONALITIES

Dane Clark
Jeanne Crain
Yvonne De Carlo

June Haver
Angela Lansbury
Peter Lawford

Lizabeth Scott
Lawrence Tierney

LEADING BOX-OFFICE ATTRACTIONS

Humphrey Bogart
Gary Cooper
Bing Crosby
Judy Garland

Greer Garson
Betty Grable
Bob Hope
Van Johnson

Margaret O'Brien
Roy Rogers
Spencer Tracy

WHAT A YEAR IT WAS!

"GOING MY WAY"

SWEEPS NEW YORK CITY'S FILM CRITICS AWARDS

(BEST PICTURE 1944)

● ● ●

Best Picture
Going My Way
Best Actor
Barry Fitzgerald
Best Director
Leo McCarey

Bing Crosby Yanked Off Golf Course To Attend Academy Awards® Ceremonies Without His Toupee

OSCAR TICKET $12.00

ACADEMY AWARDS® CEREMONY HELD AT GRAUMAN'S CHINESE ON MARCH 15, 1945
(HONORS GIVEN OUT FOR THE PAST YEAR)

Best Picture	GOING MY WAY
Best Actor	Bing Crosby, GOING MY WAY
Best Actress	Ingrid Bergman, GASLIGHT
Best Director	Leo McCarey, GOING MY WAY
Best Supporting Actor	Barry Fitzgerald, GOING MY WAY
Best Supporting Actress	Ethel Barrymore, NONE BUT THE LONELY HEART
Best Song	"Swinging On A Star," GOING MY WAY

THE OSCARS FOR 1945 "AND THE WINNER IS..."

Best Picture	THE LOST WEEKEND
Best Actor	Ray Milland, THE LOST WEEKEND
Best Actress	Joan Crawford, MILDRED PIERCE
Best Director	Billy Wilder, THE LOST WEEKEND
Best Supporting Actor	James Dunn, A TREE GROWS IN BROOKLYN
Best Supporting Actress	Anne Revere, NATIONAL VELVET
Best Song	"It Might As Well Be Spring," STATE FAIR

1945

The Outlaw

Moviegoing public finally sees pin-up queen **Jane Russell** on screen when Howard Hughes' film "The Outlaw" is released.

Boris Karloff Hired For Horror Show By RKO

MOVIE TICKET 15¢

MOVIE BOX-OFFICE RECEIPTS REACH RECORD HIGH

CANADA HONORS HOLLYWOOD WAR ACTIVITIES

Canadian ambassador addresses those gathered to pay tribute to the movie industry's War Activities and Hollywood Victory Committees.

Shirley Temple *(left)* and Margaret O'Brien *(right)* are two of the Hollywood stars in attendance.

Representatives of the film industry accept the awards for their cooperation and assistance.

Free sample package—crammed full of jobs!

C. W. POST had real Yankee ingenuity — and dyspepsia.

His dyspepsia made him dread the lead-heavy breakfasts of the '90s. His ingenuity led him to work out Grape-Nuts—a cereal that made possible a light, tempting breakfast with plenty of nourishment.

Though forty and a semi-invalid, he saw a business in Grape-Nuts. But people laughed at his new "side line" and called him a food crank. So Post was finally driven to giving Grape-Nuts away! Samples were passed out door-to-door—and families began learning how wonderfully good Grape-Nuts were!

From that faltering start, Post built Grape-Nuts up into a nationwide business. And as the business grew, it made new jobs. Not just for the people who made Grape-Nuts, but a chain of jobs. Work for farmers who grew the grain, work for shippers and handlers, for salesmen, grocers, and warehouse men.

Right now, postwar employment is America's biggest social and economic worry — employment for all the millions who want to work.

Where are the jobs coming from? Most people believe they should come from business. From businesses, large and small, which have plans for expansion on old products and have new products ready to launch. From new industries that will be born of the war—and from the filling station that's going to blossom into a garage.

This is the way to put America to work—and keep it working. But real success will depend on giving business a fair break. Rules and regulations are necessary; but they should be the sort that encourage and offer incentive to business initiative.

Unless they do this—unless business is encouraged to develop and expand—the alternative is probably jobs made up by government relief projects—perhaps including even your job.

The way you think things should be handled will have a lot to do with your future. For through your opinions and your representatives, you help make the rules under which business must operate.

Remember this... and as any legislative measure arises which might affect jobs, make the answer to this question the basis of your stand upon it: "Will this measure result in making more jobs the way Americans want their jobs made?"

On your decision may depend your future opportunity—your future job.

A Step Toward Making Jobs

Do you know about C.E.D.—the Committee for Economic Development?

It is a nonprofit, nonpolitical organization, formed two years ago by American businessmen. Its purpose is to encourage every business, large or small, to plan boldly and prepare *now* for the production and distribution of needed civilian goods . . . and thus to speed reconversion and provide postwar employment without serious interruption.

General Foods is working with C.E.D., and urges that you do, too. There are C.E.D. committees in 2800 counties and communities. Whether you have a factory, store, or other business, your local committee will give you all possible help in carrying on your postwar planning. Check with C.E.D. *now.*

 GRAPE-NUTS IS A PRODUCT OF GENERAL FOODS—AND AMERICAN ENTERPRISE

COmic relief

New York City's Mayor Fiorello LaGuardia reads the comic strips on the radio during the newspaper strike. Today's episode is a Dick Tracy adventure.

POPULAR NETWORK PROGRAMS

radio

Bob Hope
Fibber McGee & Molly
Red Skelton
Charlie McCarthy
Jack Benny
Radio Theatre
Walter Winchell
Eddie Cantor
Abbott & Costello
Amos 'n' Andy

POPULAR DAYTIME RADIO PROGRAMS

When A Girl Marries
Portia Faces Life
Ma Perkins
Breakfast In Hollywood
Romance Of Helen Trent
Pepper Young's Family
Young Widder Brown
Our Gal Sunday
Stella Dallas

Frank Sinatra Quits The Lucky Strike Hit Parade
· · · · · · · · · · · · · · · · ·
Danny Kaye Gets His Own Radio Show After Being On The Air Only Eight Times In Five Years

AIRING YOUR PROBLEMS A.A. STYLE

First radio series featuring members of Alcoholics Anonymous debuts in Detroit.

IN THE LABORATORIES *of the world's largest radio manu-facturer, the research of Philco scientists and engineers has produced miracles of electronic science for our fighters in the air and on land and sea. At every step of the advance on Berlin and the assault on the Jap empire, Radar and electronic equipment developed by Philco has done and is doing its part in helping to bring the day of final Victory.*

From Radar Research to Radio for your home

FINISH THE JOB — BUY WAR BONDS

IN THEIR research and production for war, the scientists and engineers of the Philco laboratories have made vital contributions to the sum of man's knowledge in electronic science. In their achievements which have played so important a part on every crucial battlefield, they have compressed a decade of scientific progress into months.

In this brilliant record of war research lies your assurance for the future . . . when the Philco laboratories turn from radar to radio for your home. For before the war, the achievements of its laboratories gave Philco an unbroken record of radio leadership for twelve straight years. And repeated surveys of post-war buying preference show that America looks to Philco for tomorrow's radio, by an average of 3 to 1 over any other make.

Yes, in radio, in FM reception, in phonograph reproduction, in television—whatever developments scientific progress may hold for the future, you may await them from the laboratories of Philco, the leader . . . in the days to come as in the past!

Philco presents Paul Whiteman, Georgia Gibbs, the Merry Macs. Sundays, 6 P.M., EWT, American Broadcasting Company.

PHILCO
Famous for Quality the World Over

RADIOS • PHONOGRAPHS • FM • TELEVISION • REFRIGERATORS • FREEZER CHESTS • AIR CONDITIONERS

television

Changes in family customs predicted when television sets become as popular as radios and telephones.

PREDICTIONS:

- The American family will spend more time together.
- Automobiles will be used less.
- Reading will diminish.
- People will stop talking on the telephone.

13 Channels Allocated To Commercial Television Broadcasting

Army-Navy Football Game Relayed To New York By Cable From Municipal Stadium In Philadelphia

Television Moves Closer To Establishing Entertainment And Educational Service

MUSIC

BebOp
comes into vogue

Recording Stars

**Betty Hutton
Johnnie Johnston
Stan Kenton
King Cole Trio
Tex Ritter
Andy Russell
Jo Stafford**

JOHNNY MERCER'S HITS:

- *Ac-cent-tchu-ate the Positive*
- *Sentimental Journey*
- *The Atchison, Topeka and the Santa Fe*

"Rum & Coca-Cola," a catchy calypso song by Lord Invader (Rupert Grant) and recorded by the Andrews Sisters, sweeps the nation while banned by all four radio networks on the grounds the lyrics might corrupt America's youth.

PASSINGS

Jerome Kern, major U.S. composer, dies at 60. His works include "Show Boat," which spawned the American classic "Ol' Man River." Other standards are "Look for the Silver Lining," "They Didn't Believe Me," "Smoke Gets in Your Eyes" and "The Last Time I Saw Paris."

Gus Edwards, songwriter whose hits include "By the Light of the Silvery Moon," "Orange Blossom Time" and "In My Merry Oldsmobile," dies at 64.

POPULAR SONGS

A Little On The Lonely Side
Bell Bottom Trousers
CHICKERY CHICK
Don't Fence Me In
Dream
I Dream Of You
IF I LOVED YOU
I'll Buy That Dream
I'LL WALK ALONE
I'm Beginning To See The Light
I'm Gonna Love That Guy
I'M MAKING BELIEVE

IT MIGHT AS WELL BE SPRING
It's Been A Long, Long Time
LAURA
My Dreams Are Getting Better All The Time
Rum And Coca-Cola
Saturday Night Is The Loneliest Night In The Week
That's For Me
There Goes That Song Again
The Trolley Song
Till The End Of Time
TOGETHER

WHAT A YEAR IT WAS!

DO I HEAR A SONG?

Republic Studio builds largest music-recording stage in the industry, accommodating 100-piece orchestra with a separate room for the vocalist.

⭐ Cecil B. DeMille ousted from A.F. of L.'s American Federation of Radio Artists for failure to pay $1.00 assessment and loses job on Lux Radio Theater.

⭐ Bill Goodwin is featured comedian on the Frank Sinatra Show after walking off the Burns & Allen Show.

DANCE

FOX TROT #1 DANCE— RUMBA #2

Ballroom Dancing Taught In Public Schools And Settlement Houses

Prokofiev's Ballet "Cinderella" Performed In Moscow

Ballet Companies Play To Larger Audiences

Martha Graham's Modern Dance Enjoys Triumphant World Tour

Ballet Russe de Monte Carlo Premieres Four George Balanchine Ballets:
- **Ballet Imperial**
- **Dance Concertantes**
- **Concert Barocco**
- **Mozartiana**

1945 ADVERTISEMENT

"There's something extra special on the radio tonight!"

Give a drink the benefit of Paul Jones, and it takes on a character all its own. Its subtle smoothness and full, rich flavor make it truly a flawless highball. We suggest you try Paul Jones. Soon! *Blended whiskey — 86 proof 65% grain neutral spirits. Frankfort Distillers Corporation, New York City.*

Paul Jones
...a distinguished whiskey since 1865

THEATER

BROADWAY HITS

Anna Lucasta
Bloomer Girl
Follow The Girls
Harvey
I Remember Mama
Life With Father
Oklahoma!
Song Of Norway
The Voice Of The Turtle

A TOUCHY MATTER

Mayor LaGuardia exercises censoring license and closes "Trio," a play dealing with lesbianism.

NEW YORK DRAMA CRITICS AWARD

(Best Play of the Year):
THE GLASS MENAGERIE

Rodgers & Hammerstein Debut **CAROUSEL** In New York

Camus' **CALIGULA** Premieres In Paris

BROADWAY OPENINGS
(a sampling)

A BELL FOR ADANO	ON THE TOWN	The Girl From Nantucket
A LADY SAYS YES	PYGMALION	The Hasty Heart
CAROUSEL	Star Spangled Family	The Mermaids Singing
Dark Of The Moon	STATE OF THE UNION	THE RED MILL
Dream Girl	THE ASSASSIN	THE TEMPEST
HAMLET	THE BARRETTS OF WIMPOLE STREET	Up In Central Park
Marriage Is For Single People	The Deep Mrs. Sykes	

Leonard Bernstein Brightest Young Man In The American Musical World

Zurich Acquires Villa Wesendonck — Home of Exiled Richard Wagner

Classical Music

Record Number Of Europeans Attend Concerts To Relieve Stress Of War

Goebbels Tightens Grip On Music In Vienna

Serge Prokofiev Creates "Fifth Symphony" – One Of His Greatest Works

Benjamin Britten's Opera "Peter Grimes" Premieres At The Sadler's Wells Theatre

Arnold Schönberg's New Works – "Ode To Napoleon" and "Piano Concerto" – Given First Performances As Composer Turns 70

BARITONE ROBERT MERRILL DEBUTS AT METROPOLITAN OPERA

RICHARD STRAUSS COMPOSES OPERA, "METAMORPHOSEN"

Tommy Dorsey, the sentimental gentleman of Swing, makes his classical debut with the New York City Symphony under the direction of Leopold Stokowski.

Leopold Stokowski Signs A 3-Year Contract To Conduct The Musical Activities Of The Hollywood Bowl

• • • PASSINGS • • •

Pietro Mascagni, Italian operatic composer, dies at 81.

Hungarian composer, **Bela Bartok**, dies at 64 in New York City. Hired by Columbia University to transcribe Yugoslavian folk music, Bartok will best be remembered for his "Piano Concertos 1 and 2," "Violin Concerto 2" and his provocative, less understood composition "Concerto for Orchestra."

WHAT A YEAR IT WAS!

1945 ADVERTISEMENT

IF SCHOOL KIDS can sneak a snack, why can't teacher? Any time's the time for Wheaties, that famous "Breakfast of Champions"! At breakfast—or whenever you're just plain hungry—shake out a big bowlful. Top your crackly whole wheat flakes with milk and fruit. And have fun. (Keep the package close by—Wheaties are second-helping good, as many a champ could tell you.) Nourishing? Flakes of *whole wheat*, this General Mills product. Had your Wheaties today?

BOOKS

PULITZER PRIZE WINNERS

BIOGRAPHY
Russell Blaine Nye
George Bancroft: Brahmin Rebel

HISTORY
Stephen Bonsal
Unfinished Business

NOVEL
John Hersey
A Bell For Adano

AMERICAN POETRY
Karl Jay Shapiro
V-Letter and Other Poems

NOBEL PRIZE WINNER

LITERATURE
Gabriela Mistral

BOOKS OF 1945

A Lion Is In The Streets
Adria Locke Langley

Animal Farm
George Orwell

An Intelligent American's Guide To The Peace
Sumner Welles

Battle Report
Cmdr. Walter Karig & Lt. Welbourn Kelley

Black Boy
Richard Wright

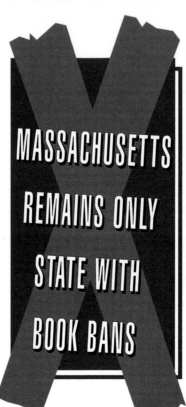

MASSACHUSETTS REMAINS ONLY STATE WITH BOOK BANS

BOOKS OF 1945

Brave Men
Ernie Pyle

Brideshead Revisited
Evelyn Waugh

Caesar And Christ
Will Durant

Cannery Row
John Steinbeck

Cass Timberlane
Sinclair Lewis

Christ Stopped At Eboli
Carlo Levi

Daisy Kenyon
Elizabeth Janeway

Das Glasperlenspiel
Hermann Hesse

Dragon Harvest
Upton Sinclair

Forever Amber
Kathleen Winsor

Forever China
Robert Payne

Glory For Me
MacKinlay Kantor

BOOKS OF 1945

Great Son
Edna Ferber

Harvey
(Pulitzer Prize Winner)
Mary Chase

Here Is Your War
Ernie Pyle

Image Of Josephine
Booth Tarkington

Immortal Wife
Irving Stone

I Never Left Home
Bob Hope

**L'Age de Raison
Les Sursis**
Jean-Paul Sartre

Leave Her To Heaven
Ben Ames Williams

Left Hand, Right Hand
Osbert Sitwell

**Lincoln
The President**
J.G. Randall

Loving
Henry Green

Poor Child
Anne Parish

Portrait Of Marriage
Pearl S. Buck

Prater Violet
Christopher Isherwood

SCHOLARLY WORKS

The Free State
D.W. Brogan

World War: Its Cause And Cure
L.G. Curtis

The Anatomy of Courage
Lord Moran

For The Sake Of Heaven
Martin Buber

Religion In America
William L. Sperry

Religious Experience
C.J. Webb

• PASSINGS •

Ellen Glasgow, author of the Pulitzer Prize winning book, *In This Our Life*, dies in Richmond, Virginia at 71.

Humorist **Robert Benchley** dies at 56 from a cerebral hemorrhage.

Theodore Dreiser, author of *An American Tragedy*, dies at 74.

French poet, **Paul Valery**, dies.

BOOKS OF 1945

River Road
Frances Parkinson Keyes

Stuart Little
E.B. White

The Age Of Jackson
Arthur M. Schlesinger, Jr.

The Egg And I
Betty MacDonald

The Friendly Persuasion
Jessamyn West

The Green Years
A.J. Cronin

The Pursuit Of Love
Nancy Mitford

The Razor's Edge
W. Somerset Maugham

The Robe
Lloyd C.Douglas

The Thurber Carnival
James Thurber

The Wayfarers
Dan Wickendon

The World Of Washington Irving
Van Wyck Brooks

Try And Stop Me
Bennett Cerf

Up Front
Bill Mauldin

When Democracy Builds
Frank Lloyd Wright

ART

ART TREASURES SURVIVE THE WAR

Despite the vast amount of destruction of architectural monuments in Europe, great care was taken in both Italy and France to protect historic art treasures by removing them from museums and hiding them in places of safety.

The American Commission for the Protection and Salvage of Artistic and Historic Monuments aided the restoration by erecting temporary roofs on bombed structures to protect frescoes and other art objects from the perils of weather.

Art treasures stolen by the Nazis were recovered all over Europe, with the largest discovery made at Neuschwanstein Castle where priceless treasures from the Rothschild, Kann and Stern French collections were hidden, set aside for Hermann Goering's private collection. Over 2,000 works of art were discovered in a German iron mine taken when France was invaded. Generals Patton, Bradley and Eisenhower viewed the priceless works valued at approximately $200 million.

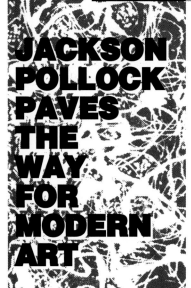

JACKSON POLLOCK PAVES THE WAY FOR MODERN ART

 Stanley Spencer Continues His Series "Resurrection"

 Henry Moore Sculpts "Family Group"

 Stuart Davis Paints "For Internal Use Only," An Abstract Painting

 Max Weber Paints "Brass Band," An Expressionist Painting

Aerial Photography Provides A Dramatic And Unprecedented Extension Of The Visual Experience

French intellectuals meet at Pablo Picasso's Left Bank studio in support of the overthrow of dictator Francisco Franco

 Georgia O'Keefe Most Famous Woman Painter In The U.S.

 Francis Guy Is Dubbed Grandfather Of U.S. Landscape Painting

✦ **José Maria Velasco hailed as one of the great modern landscape painters 33 years after his death.**

✦ **Pablo Picasso hails Winston Churchill's painting of a red brick Riviera villa as the work of a professional.**

✦ **Rubens' "Holy Family" discovered in an underground cave in Siegen, Germany by U.S. troops.**

Largest exhibition of paintings by Claude Monet ever assembled held by Wildenstein Gallery in New York

WHAT A YEAR IT WAS!

"Nothing fits except the Camels"

It's a wonderful feeling, isn't it, Soldier? You slip out of that G.I. shirt—*well, anyway I washed it in the Rhine.* You give those heavy boots a meaningful toss into the corner—*when I think of the miles, and the mud* ... And then you reach for that soft white shirt, those blessedly comfortable slacks—*I never thought I'd see the day!* You're home again, Soldier!

You may find those old "civvies" don't quite fit ... may find many things a little different ... but this you can be sure of: The Camels you get here at home will be the same mild, flavorful cigarette of costlier tobaccos you knew so well over there. War or Peace, Camels are still Camels. And with Camels, it's still *the service first* ... until you, all of you, are back again ... for keeps.

 This button signifies that the wearer has been honorably discharged from the armed services of the United States.

CAMEL
TURKISH & DOMESTIC BLEND CIGARETTES

CHOICE QUALITY

THE "T-ZONE"

—Taste and Throat—that's the final proving ground of any cigarette. Only your taste and throat can decide which cigarette tastes best to *you* ... and how it affects your throat. Based on the experience of millions of smokers, we believe that Camels will suit your "T-ZONE" to a "T."

◄ The Service First

Army, Navy, Marines, and Coast Guard—wherever they are, wherever they go, they have first call on Camels.

R. J. Reynolds Tobacco Company, Winston-Salem, N. C.

154

❏ **U.S. Abstractionist Stuart Davis Gives A Full-Dress Showing At New York's Museum Of Modern Art**

❏ **The Albany Institute Of History And Art Organizes "The Negro Artist Comes Of Age" Acknowledging The Growing Importance Of Negro Artists**

❏ **New York's Guggenheim Museum Announces Plans To Build A Cylindrical Museum At Central Park & 89th Street Designed By Frank Lloyd Wright**

Sir John Tenniel's "Alice Through The Looking-Glass" and other drawings put on the auction block in Manhattan

CRITICS CHOICE IN CONTEMPORARY U.S. ART
(a sampling)

William Thon
"Under the Brooklyn Bridge"

Charles Kilgore
"The Day Ends"

Fred Conway
"Kids"

Jon Corbino
"The Family"

Nathaniel Jacobson
"Ezekiel"

Clarence Carter
"Marsha"

John McCrady
"Our Daily Bread"

Ben Shahn
"The Quartet"

PASSINGS

Alexander Stirling Calder, whose works are included in the permanent collections of the Pennsylvania Academy of Fine Arts, the Smithsonian Institution, the Metropolitan Museum and the Museum of Modern Art in New York City, dies at 74. Among his most renowned works is the Washington figure for the arch in New York's Washington Square.

Rene Lalique, French designer of jewelry and glassware, dies at 85.

Max Kalish, U.S. sculptor, dies at 54. Among his notable pieces are statues of Christ and Lincoln.

This "Gay, New-Day Kitchen" can be Yours!

Out of the Past . . . It popped right out of a Pennsylvania Dutch hope chest . . . and did you ever see a more entrancing idea for a kitchen? Hearts and flowers and furbelows carefully copied in colors that sing their saucy way into a modern step-saving setting.

Into the Present . . . Here's a picture of planned kitchen efficiency. Streamlined design that starts with plenty of working surface . . . and a "tri-angular" refrigerator-range-sink arrangement that hops, skips and jumps you through meal making. There's a planning desk, too, for recipe books and kitchen "bookkeeping" . . . and a built-in upholstered seat with storage drawers underneath. Pull up a movable utility table and there's your family breakfast corner!

Its Kelvinator Refrigerator . . . slides snugly into the corner near the window . . . big, roomy and beautiful. There will be different zones of cold for all kinds of perishable foods. A frozen food compartment to hold a roast, keep frozen fruits and vegetables for weeks.

A Cold-Mist Freshener compartment, walled off with shining glass, to crisp up greens, keep uncovered leftovers flavorful.

Its Kelvinator Electric Range . . . puts joy into cooking! Completely automatic . . . it starts breakfast while you're still asleep . . . cooks whole dinners by itself. Helps you serve tastier, more nutritious meals because electric cookery conserves more goodness . . . more vitamins. Helps you keep your kitchen cool as a cucumber during July and August dog days.

heart of *your home* **Kelvinator**
of NASH-KELVINATOR CORPORATION

Refrigerators • Electric Ranges • Home Freezers • Electric
Water Heaters • Beverage Coolers • Ice Cream Cabinets
Frozen Food Merchandisers • Commercial Refrigerating Units

Its Kelvinator Home Freezer . . . completes the setting. A treasure-chest to dip into all year 'round for all kinds of in-season foods and out-of-season luxuries . . . tender young chickens, choice meats, fish, game, fruits and succulent vegetables from your summer garden. Enables you to plan and buy months ahead.

It's for You . . . if Pennsylvania Dutch decoration makes you tingle with excitement. But, perhaps your imagination paints a picture of *you* in a French Provincial, Modern, Ranch House, Cape Cod or English setting. Complete details and color sketches by America's leading small-home architects for building these six beautiful, efficient kitchens are yours for the asking in a wonderful new free booklet, "Kelvinator in the Home of Your Dreams." See your Kelvinator Retailer today, or drop a post card for your copy to Dept. 9-E, Kelvinator, Detroit 32, Mich.

Tune In ♪

Nash-Kelvinator's hit musical program Sundays 4:30 p.m., E.W.T. Blue Network.

Registered Nurses! Wounded men need you! Join the Army Nurse Corps now! War collect! Surgeon General, U. S. Army, Washington, D. C.

F A S H I O N

Leg make-up is used as an alternative to rayon and cotton stockings, with fake seams drawn on the leg with an eyebrow pencil.

With restrictions against extravagant ruffles, pleats and full sleeves, designers display wonderful ingenuity in creating styles using the limited amounts of available materials, with the wrap-around skirt being a prime example.

Swimsuits are covered up with the cholo, a loose-swinging coat influenced by a Peruvian design.

Nylon becomes popular after the war and spawns creation of Wash-And-Wear dresses.

The Wing Sleeve Becomes Popular

Coats And Suits Discard Their Collars

With the end of the war, clothes begin to take on a more relaxed, glamorous look and luxurious brocaded coats and embroidered, sequined evening gowns are again possible.

flat Shoes More Popular Than Heels

THE AMERICAN MALE LOOK

The military uniform is the predominant look during most of the year. The popular off-duty dress is a crew neck sweater with shirt, tie and jacket. Lounge suits grow in popularity and are available in single and double breasted styles. The hair is worn short with hats an integral part of every man's wardrobe.

CHRISTIAN DIOR SPARKS CONTROVERSY WITH THE CREATION OF HIS "NEW LOOK"

While Christian Dior is being celebrated by fashion magazine editors for his revolutionary "New Look" which emphasizes rounded bosoms, shoulders and hips, longer skirts and tiny waistlines, American men are up in arms about the cost of replacing their lady's entire wardrobe as well as protesting the disappearance of their legs. Some women don't take the change lying down as they sign petitions against lowering their hemlines.

"Too bad, Bob, you can't keep yours on, too!"

The Stetson she admires so much is "The Whippet"

IT'S only natural for a woman to notice and comment on the clothes a man wears—especially if he's as well-dressed as the fellow above.

Every detail of his outfit is right for the occasion.

The medium gray worsted suit and soft white collar indicate quiet good taste—the green-and-gray tie, a touch of imagination.

An appropriate crowning touch is supplied by the Royal Stetson "Whippet". The willow green felt harmonizes with the gray suit and gray-green tie; the smartly bound edge and conservative lines complete the note of semi-formality.

In this combination, you can be sure of looking well, and feeling at ease, on any dress-up occasion.

And whatever the occasion or the clothing you're wearing, remember this: there's a style and color of Stetson perfectly suited to them.

The Royal Stetson "Whippet" illustrated above is priced at $10. Other Stetson hats are priced to $40. John B. Stetson Company, U. S. and Canada...makers of hats for men and women.

. . .

P. S. Remember, loose talk still costs lives...keep it under your Stetson.

You'll look your best in the right

STETSON

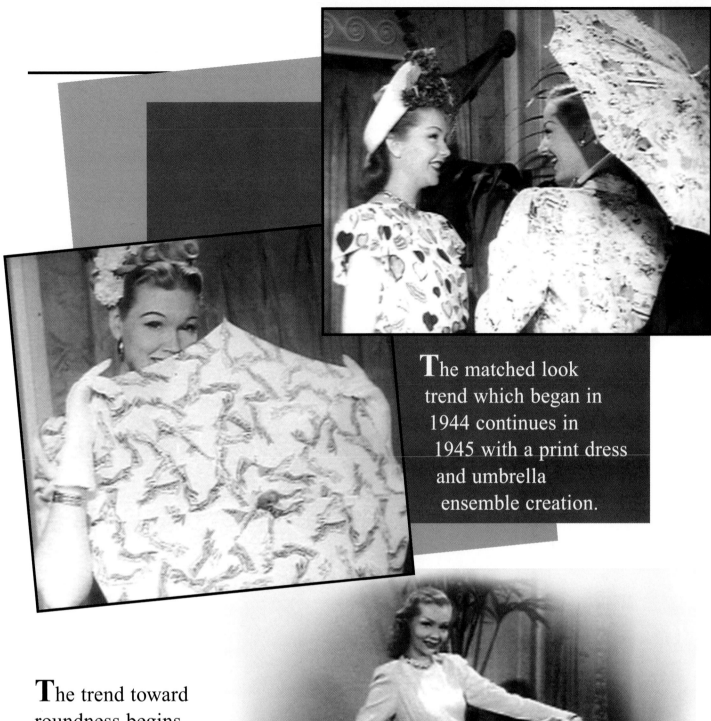

The matched look trend which began in 1944 continues in 1945 with a print dress and umbrella ensemble creation.

The trend toward roundness begins early in the year with the introduction of the tight, corseted midriff and softer, fuller skirts.

Bobby-soxers drink Cokes, prefer to be called "Teen Timers" and wear monogrammed blouses with matching dirndl skirts.

Rick-rack trim, charm bracelets and pigtails are popular with the 11-17 year-olds.

Another Look: *Jerseys and Belted Skirts*

162

What's Charlie got that you haven't?

1. If you think we're going to say that Charlie is a wow because he wears the clothes shown below — including that Royal Stetson Whippet — you're wrong.

No, Charlie is a success because of the kind of fellow he is.

But, *being* that kind of fellow, Charlie is very thoughtful about being dressed correctly for the occasion.

For example, take a close-up look at that blue-gray suit and topcoat he's wearing...

2. Charlie knows that a worsted suit and covert topcoat aren't an open sesame to social success. But he also knows that for dress-up occasions they're tops in taste.

3. Charlie chose that white shirt and that red-and-blue tie to add a little warmth to the proceedings. And, of course, gray gloves and black shoes are right on the button.

4. To top this outfit, Charlie picked the Royal Stetson Whippet, in Caribou Gray. Medium proportions and smart styling make it right for any semi-formal occasion. It's $10.

Right for stepping out — The Royal STETSON Whippet

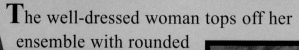

The rounded silhouette, tight at the throat, wrists and waist is the new look.

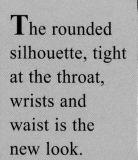

The well-dressed woman tops off her ensemble with rounded hats made of felt and crocheted wool, trimmed with flowers and netting.

Hairstyles vary from being swept up into topknots, or little knots at the nape of the neck. Ribbons, clusters of flowers or bands of metal are laced through these hairdos.

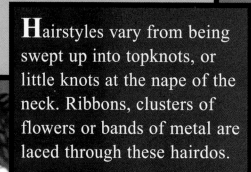

OUT OF THE MOTHBALLS

THE MILITARY LOOK INFLUENCES FASHION

A modified version of the Eisenhower Jacket becomes a ladies' fashion statement.

The Canadienne, a three-quarter length coat originating in Paris, is adapted from the Canadian soldier's coat.

The military look is evident in this sailor dress and matching cap.

Women are putting on their pretty party dresses made of satin, taffeta, lace and faille for the first time in five years for afternoon cocktails or tea dances. To achieve a tiny look at the waist, women wear stiff farthingales underneath their gowns.

The British sailor cap influenced this hat.

SPORTS

OUTSTANDING ATHLETES OF THE YEAR

MALE
Byron Nelson
No. 1 Golfer For Second Year After Taking 18 Major Tournaments
— Wins A Record $64,600 In War Bonds —

FEMALE
Mrs. Mildred (Babe) Didrikson Zaharias
Retains Western Open Title

DAILY

CIRCULATION 3

CHAMPIONS

BILLIARDS

WORLD THREE CUSHION
Welker Cochran, San Francisco

WORLD POCKET
Willie Mosconi, Toledo

CHESS

WORLD
Dr. Alexandre Alekhine, Paris

SOCCER

NATIONAL CHALLENGE CUP
Brookhattan, New York

ICE SKATING

WOMEN'S NORTH AMERICAN
Barbara Ann Scott, Ottawa

WOMEN'S NATIONAL
Gretchen Merrill, Boston

SWIMMING

FREE-STYLE
Ann Curtis, San Francisco
6 National Titles

WHAT A YEAR IT WAS!

BASEBALL

WORLD SERIES

Detroit Tigers defeat Chicago Cubs 4 games to 3, with the third game producing the greatest pitching ever seen in a World Series.

HANK GREENBERG
World Series Hero

MOST VALUABLE PLAYERS

AMERICAN LEAGUE

PLAYER	TEAM
HAL NEWHOUSER	**Tigers**
— Followed in voting by —	
EDDIE MAYO	Tigers
GEORGE STIRNWEISS	Yankees
DAVID FERRISS	Red Sox
GEORGE MYATT	Senators
VERN STEPHENS	Browns
ROGER WOLFF	Senators
LOU BOUDREAU	Indians
GEORGE CASE	Senators
PAUL RICHARDS	Tigers

NATIONAL LEAGUE

PLAYER	TEAM
PHIL CAVARRETTA	**Cubs**
— Followed in voting by —	
TOMMY HOLMES	Braves
CHARLES BARRETT	Cards
ANDY PAFKO	Cubs
GEORGE KUROWSKI	Cards
HANK BOROWY	Cubs
HANK WYSE	Cubs
MARTY MARION	Cards
DIXIE WALKER	Dodgers
GOODIE ROSEN	Dodgers

Babe Ruth, "Sultan of Swat," Announces New Career As A Wrestling Referee

New York Yankees Sold To Syndicate Controlled By Lawrence MacPhail, Del Webb And Dan Topping For An Estimated $2.8 Million

Branch Rickey, Walter O'Malley And John L. Smith Acquire Controlling Interest In Brooklyn Dodgers

Baseball Enjoys Record-Breaking Attendance

ORGANIZED BASEBALL HIRES FIRST NEGRO* PLAYER

Babe Ruth, "Sultan of Swat," Turns 51

OCTOBER 23:

Jack Roosevelt "Jackie" Robinson, a Georgia-born player from the Kansas City Monarchs of the Negro League, will join the Montreal club, a Brooklyn Dodgers affiliate in the International League. Robinson, son of a sharecropper and grandson of a slave, was a four-sport star at U.C.L.A. and made All-American as halfback.

*Negro was the commonly used term in 1945.

The Annual Major League All-Star Game Is Not Played This Year Because Of Government Travel Restrictions

ONE-ARMED BASEBALL PLAYER INSPIRATION TO ALL

One-armed Pete Gray of the St. Louis Browns is this season's sensation. Pete lost his arm when he was six, but never lost his determination to make the big league.

Pete played two years for Memphis and came to the big leagues on his own merit. His batting average is good but most of his hits are singles.

Pete's success is a lesson in pursuing your dream no matter what hardships you must overcome.

THE FIGHTING IRISH TAKE ON N.Y.U.

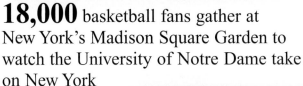

18,000 basketball fans gather at New York's Madison Square Garden to watch the University of Notre Dame take on New York University.

N.Y.U. stabs at the basket, but Notre Dame grabs the ball, comes down court, and scores the final shot, winning 66-60.

 # COLLEGE BASKETBALL

National Intercollegiate Champions
OKLAHOMA AGGIES

Five Members Of The Brooklyn College Basketball Team Suspended For Accepting Bribes

RED CROSS PLAY-OFF CHAMPS

Western Conference
Iowa State University
Eastern Intercollegiate League
Pennsylvania State

1945
FOOTBALL

Cleveland Rams Defeat Washington Redskins 15-14 For NFL Championship

The Eleventh Airborne Division Beats The Forty-First Division 25-12 In The Tokyo Bowl

Pro Football Fans Set All-Time Attendance Record

NFL Player Of The Year:
BOB WATERFIELD
CLEVELAND RAMS

POSTWAR FOOTBALL UNIFORMS TO OFFER GREATER PROTECTION FROM INJURY

Postwar football uniforms will boast eight pounds less armor and will incorporate fiber glass jerseys, nylon pants and foam rubber pads for greater protection.

NATIONAL COLLEGE FOOTBALL CHAMPIONS:

Army Beats Navy 32-13 In 18th Consecutive Win In Two Seasons – Ranked Among All-Time Great Teams

HEISMAN TROPHY WINNER:
Felix Blanchard, *Fullback, Army*

COLLEGE FOOTBALL

Alabama Chosen Ahead Of Navy As Season's Runner-Up

Southern California Trojans Trounce Tennessee Volunteers 25-0 And Win Rose Bowl

TENNIS

U.S. LAWN TENNIS SINGLES CHAMPIONS

MEN: *U.S. Army Sergeant,* **FRANK A. PARKER**

WOMEN: **Mrs. SARAH PALFREY COOKE**

Sgt. Joe Louis, Undefeated Heavyweight Champion Of The World, Returns To The U.S. After His Overseas Tour

EDDIE ARCARO Wins Third Kentucky Derby Riding "Hoop Jr." And Wins Belmont Stakes Riding "Pavot"

W.D. WRIGHT Rides "Polynesian" To Preakness Win

LOUIS B. MAYER'S "Busher" Wins Hollywood Derby $50,000 Purse

Tracks Reopen May 12 – Season Ends As Most Amazing In History

Harness Horse Of The Year: **"Titan Hanover"**

HORSE RACING

BOXING

Boxer Of The Year: **Rocky Graziano**

Welterweight **Sugar Ray Robinson** Beats Middleweight **Jake La Motta** In Madison Square Garden Bout

HOCKEY

Toronto Maple Leafs Win Hockey's Stanley Cup

WHAT A YEAR IT WAS!

1945 WAS A GREAT YEAR, BUT...

THE BEST IS YET TO COME!

PHOTOGRAPHY CREDITS

All photographs are courtesy of **FlikBaks**™ unless they are credited below.
The author gratefully acknowledges the following contributions:

Page

9	Courtesy of AT&T Archives
16	Courtesy of The Coca-Cola Company
24	Courtesy of The Andrew Jergens Company
28	Left : Courtesy of Westpoint Stevens
	Right: Courtesy of Chesebrough Pond's USA Co.
31	Courtesy of Mobil Corporation
39	Courtesy of Liggett Group Inc.
42	Courtesy of Mobil Corporation
50	Courtesy of Greyhound Lines, Inc.
59	Courtesy of Navistar International Transportation Corp.
60	Speech reprinted courtesy of **FlikBaks**™
73	Courtesy of The Boeing Company
76	Courtesy of The General Electric Company
79	Courtesy of Nestle USA, Inc.
94	Courtesy of Johnson & Johnson
96	Courtesy of Gerber Products Company
105	Courtesy of Kimberly-Clark Corporation
109	Courtesy of Maytag Corp.
115	Courtesy of Campbell Soup Company
119	Courtesy of Chesebrough Pond's USA Co.
121	Courtesy of Nestle USA, Inc.
123	Courtesy of Wyeth-Ayerst Laboratories
128	From the collections of Henry Ford Museum & Greenfield Village
130	Courtesy of Borden, Inc.
137	Courtesy of Allied Artists Entertainment, Inc.
139	Courtesy of Kraft General Foods
142	Courtesy of Philips Consumer Electronics
146	Reprinted with permission of Joseph E. Seagram & Sons, Inc. and Heaven Hill Distilleries, Inc.
149	Courtesy of General Mills Archives
151	Courtesy Doubleday & Co., Inc.
156	Courtesy of White Consolidated Industries, Inc.
159	Courtesy of The Florsheim Shoe Company
160	Reprinted with permission of the John B. Stetson Company
163	Reprinted with permission of the John B. Stetson Company
166	Courtesy of Whitman's Candies, Inc.